THE TIME-OUT PRESCRIPTION

THE TIME-OUT PRESCRIPTION

PRESCRIPTION

A Parent's Guide to
Positive and Loving Discipline

DONNA G. CORWIN

CONTEMPORARY BOOKS
A TRIBUNE COMPANY

Library of Congress Cataloging-in-Publication Data

Corwin, Donna G.
    The time-out prescription : a parent's guide to positive and
loving discipline / Donna G. Corwin
        p.   cm.
    Includes index.
    ISBN 0-8092-3235-9
    1. Discipline of children.   2. Timeout method.   3. Child
rearing.
    HQ770.4.C67   1996
    649'.64—dc20   96-13811
                                                                 CIP

Cover design by Monica Baziuk
Cover photo copyright © 1986 Joseph E. Mozdzen/Photobank, Inc.
Back cover author photo by Terri Sigal
Interior design by Mary Ballachino

Published by Contemporary Books
An imprint of NTC/Contemporary Publishing Company
Two Prudential Plaza, Chicago, Illinois 60601-6790
Manufactured in the United States of America
International Standard Book Number: 0-8092-3235-9
10   9   8   7   6   5   4   3   2   1

To Alexandra — my precious daughter

Contents

Foreword

"Time-out" has become a household word. We use it in so many contexts. For the athlete, time-out is the coach's way of helping his or her players regroup or devise a fresh strategy. When time-out is used properly, it is as helpful and effective for the parent-child relationship as it is for the coach-athlete relationship.

Time-out's usefulness was recently brought home to me when Wendy, a mother in one of my parenting workshops, reported "losing it" with her four-year-old son, Jason, after a particularly stressful day and baby Lydia's earache. "A few minutes after my yelling at him," Wendy said, "Jason came over to me and put his arm around my shoulder and said, 'Mommy, I think you could use a time-out.' Instantly, I responded, 'You're right, honey! Mommy *really* could use a time-out.' I then proceeded to take a few minutes for myself—collecting myself." Wendy was thrilled at how simple and effective time-out was for both her and Jason. She told other parents that she was even considering using a time-out when she and her husband, Bob, were "stressing."

Wendy and Jason are obviously learning that time-out is not just a discipline technique or a punishment. Time-out is best used as a strategy to defuse and correct an escalating situation without doing damage to the parent-child relationship.

The Time-Out Prescription is a straightforward, excellent book meant to help you and your child learn self-control and self-discipline by loving and positive methods.

—Mitch Golant, Ph.D.

Acknowledgments

I gratefully acknowledge and thank these people for their support:

- Kara Leverte, my editor and "time-out" co-supporter. Thank you for your suggestions and support.

- Stan Corwin, my wonderful husband, my cheerleader and adviser

- Ann Benya—thank you once again for a perfect manuscript

- The parents who so generously shared their experiences

- Craig Bolt, project editor. Thanks for your keen eye and great work on the manuscript.

Introduction

Children can be your greatest joy in life. They can also be your biggest challenge. Here is this unique, adorable, complex, thinking, feeling little child suddenly screaming, whining, saying "No," reducing you to mush. How did this happen? Why can you handle every aspect of your life with ease except for your child? Why does the discipline of your child take you into another realm of consciousness? You feel guilty, then frustrated, angry, and confused.

Raising a child is an ongoing process. You are dealing with all aspects of another person's thoughts, needs, and feelings. It is the most serious and fun job you will ever have, but you need some skills before you begin the long process of successful child rearing.

Some parents turn to discipline methods their parents used. Often the results are mixed. Most modern parents do not feel comfortable spanking their child, and "just talking" to a strong-willed child can leave you nowhere. You need alternative methods to guide you through your child's formative years.

As a parent myself and the author of numerous parenting books, I have experimented with many child-rearing techniques. That is what led me to write about the most successful methods.

When I wrote *Time-Out for Toddlers,* I had no idea what a huge following the book would have. After hundreds of conversations with parents, I saw the need for *The Time-Out Prescription,* a book that would further expand this simple hands-on approach to a remarkable discipline method.

Through my daughter's babyhood, toddlerhood, and early elementary years, I have used time-out. It is certainly one of the best discipline methods for toddlers and young children. It is a firm but nonaggressive means of helping your child respect the boundaries you set. It is also a way to set a positive role model for your child instead of spanking. Children are extremely impressionable and will emulate their parents' behavior. If the parent hits and pushes and yells, so will the child. Time-out and the other discipline methods in the book will help you avoid this parental pitfall.

As your child begins to get older, you might question whether time-out will still be effective. I certainly did. When my daughter, Alexandra, was nearing nine years old, I thought maybe she had outgrown time-out. She had always been temperamentally challenging and not often responsive to discipline in general. I guess you could say that I was not listening to my own advice, and I became lazy.

After struggling with her on a regular basis and not getting too far, I decided to go back to my parenting "roots." After all, *I* was the parenting expert, and I had lost touch with my most successful method.

One evening Alexandra and I were having a major push-pull battle of the wills over her refusing to go to bed on time.

It was a familiar argument and one that always went nowhere. The battle usually ended up with a drama— screaming, yelling, and tears. I couldn't understand why someone such as I, who had so much parenting experience, couldn't get control of this situation. In the heat of battle I yelled, "Time-out!"

Alexandra was shocked. She actually asked me, "What did you say, Mommy?" She soon found out *exactly* what I said when I pulled out our trusty old time-out chair and timer. I put the chair in the hallway and sat her down on the chair facing the corner. I told her she was getting a time-out for arguing, raising her voice, and refusing to listen.

Alexandra resisted at first. She grumbled and cried and whined. I held strong, which has never been easy for a pushover like me. But then I walked into my bedroom and let her know that I was going to take *my* time-out as well, which I needed desperately at that point. I also let her know that if she didn't take her time-out, there would be further consequences. I set the timer for nine minutes. She stood up and put her hands on her hips, then sat down. I went into my bedroom and closed the door.

After about five minutes, I peeked outside of my door. She was sitting quietly on the chair. How miraculous. How simple. Time-out still worked. I was ecstatic.

I let another four minutes elapse. The timer went off. She was ready to talk. I had calmed down, and we were both willing to listen to one another. It was so effective, and yet I had lost touch with this powerful behavioral tool.

This experience was in part the genesis for *The Time-Out Prescription*. I realized that parents need not only to begin using time-out but to *continue* using it as their children grow older.

The book is both a practical introduction to using time-out and an excellent reference for those parents who have used it but need to refresh and restart time-out again.

Time-out is the tool that can keep *both* parent and child in control. But for time-out to work, it has to be used correctly. Many parents with whom I've spoken use time-out but do so incorrectly. I am constantly getting calls from people who ask me to give them a quick working outline of time-out. Usually they aren't sure where to use it or for how long or what to do outside the home or when it might not be appropriate.

The Time-Out Prescription offers simple, practical parenting information on all aspects of time-out. You will not find a lot of elaborate theories. The book is short and to the point. Most parents don't have time to read long, drawn-out, overly analytical psychology books that leave them asking more questions than when they first began.

I am a parent. When I help you, I help myself. *The Time-Out Prescription* will guide you through each step. The book has charts and checklists that will help you double-check how effectively time-out is working for you.

Of course, using time-out in conjunction with other discipline methods is even more helpful so that you will have the benefits of both. Tools such as positive reinforcement, counting to ten, learn-to-listen skills, charting, and age-appropriate checklists can provide parents with a useful formula for loving discipline.

The book even shares answers to other parents' questions, which should help us all to understand our own problems better.

You will also find a section on your child's temperament. This is a key chapter in the book, one I consider extremely important. Every child is different. Thus, every child will respond to discipline, and specifically to time-out, differently. You can't measure your success by someone else's child. You need to explore who your child is, what his or her needs are, and how the two of you interact. The way we interact with our child is often the key to our parenting success.

The section on "family fit" will help you define the personality differences between you and your child. Often parents do not recognize that parent-child differences can negatively impact the family structure.

In *The Time-Out Prescription*, I will empower you to help your child while simultaneously helping yourself avoid constant conflict. Family respect and harmony can be a large task. With my workable technique, you will be on your way to a stronger parent-child bond, as well as feeling better about your relationship with your most precious asset—your child.

CHAPTER 1

What Is
Time-Out?

A Working Definition of Time-Out

Simply stated, time-out is an effective behavioral technique whereby your child, on misbehaving, is removed from the area and required to sit quietly for a period of time (comparable to his or her age). When the time is up, your child is taken off time-out and given a chance to start over without further repercussions. The method can be used for children ages two to ten years of age.

In sports, a time-out is called to allow the players to regroup, rethink their plays, and take a rest. The same theory holds true for your child. Children need someone to help them learn appropriate behavior and calm down. Often they don't have the ability to turn off a behavior. A child can't think "I'm having so much fun, but I need to stop and go have dinner." A toddler can go into stimulus overload and wreak havoc. This is where a time-out allows the child, like an athlete, to take a break.

What makes time-out so effective is its nonemotional way of correcting your child's behavior. When you yell or spank your child, you are investing highly charged emotions into your discipline. You may say or do something hurtful or harmful that can leave emotional scars. Time-out, if used properly, removes you from the emotionality attached to yelling and hitting. It can also keep your child from escalating the misbehavior even further.

Time-out serves the parent as well, because it also gives you a chance to calm down and rethink your actions. A parent can go into the same overload a child gets into, a combustible situation that can result in an explosion.

Why Is Time-Out Necessary?

We live in a violent society. The media bombard us with negative, angry images that our children will be exposed to, either directly or indirectly. Protecting children from everything they see, hear, and read is very difficult. Raising a moral, responsible, and caring child becomes a difficult task in a world that celebrates indiscretions with starlike attention, splashes the faces of child abusers on the pages of every media publication, and exposes all kinds of cruel behavior on talk shows.

Children get mixed messages about what is important. They see bad behavior treated with a great amount of attention. Even the bad behavior of sports heroes is highlighted

Discipline Is What We Make It

An established behavioral discipline routine lets children know the consequences of behavior before they act. Creating a familial discipline in your home is up to you. But you should follow a consistent routine. A child familiar with time-out will learn to *wait and think* before acting.

To *wait* and *think* (wait for time to pass and think before acting) are what you ultimately want to train your child to do. But this technique may take some time to learn. Young children often do not have the cognitive ability to delay behavior. Toddlers are especially impulsive; they come from the "act first, think last" school. But a consistent discipline method (time-out) that is the basis for the wait-and-think technique will eventually become second nature to children who, as they grow older (about five), will learn to delay negative behaviors on their own.

The time-out techniques are the necessary elements to raising your child in a caring, responsible, and humanistic way. You want to send the message that bad behavior is inappropriate but that there are nonphysical ways of dealing with it.

Raising a child is challenging at best. No one gets off easy, but you can create a good relationship with your child by the discipline choices you make. Time-out should be your first choice. Helping to foster good self-esteem in your child is another reason to use time-out.

Four-year-old Lisa had a habit of hitting her playmate

Devon. Every time Lisa hit Devon, Lisa's mom would slap Lisa's hand and tell her, "You are a bad little girl." When Lisa's kindergarten school teacher asked each child to say something about herself, Lisa answered, "I'm a bad girl." The teacher was shocked. She tried to explain to Lisa that people, especially little children, aren't bad. Sometimes children's *behavior* is bad because it hurts other people, but Lisa is not a bad person.

This example helps demonstrate a key factor in child discipline. Separating the child's behavior from the child is imperative.

Children are extremely impressionable and will tend to believe what you tell them. That is part of their innocent charm. They still believe in monsters and fairies. If you constantly tell a child "You are bad," then that strong message is being sent into her fragile psyche. A child who truly believes she is bad will then act out, because such children think that bad behavior is expected of them.

Children's self-esteem can be greatly hurt if they don't believe anything they do is ever good or OK. If a child has the mind-set that she is labeled a "bad child," then that is how she will view herself as she grows up.

We have many ways to send a message to our children about their behavior, and I will talk about that in the book.

What makes time-out an important tool is that it helps young children learn to *own up* to their behavior and, as they mature, to take responsibility for their actions. By this I mean that young children are highly attached to their parents. When the parent inadvertently projects behavior onto the child, that child models the parental action.

For instance, when Jake's father spanked him for disobeying, Jake turned around and spanked his two-year-old brother. This negative pattern will continue unless Jake has a positive model to follow that separates him from his behavior. Time-out works because there is no physical contact that binds parent and child in a negative interaction. Time-out immediately corrects the behavior. The child knows what she did wrong and is given time to think about it.

CHAPTER 2

The Time-Out Prescription

To use time-out properly, you will need some basic tools. Until you use these behavioral tools appropriately and consistently, you will be in time-out purgatory waiting and hoping for miraculous results with your child.

Once you get time-out down perfectly, you must be willing to use it. If this sounds odd, it's not. A mother might read dozens of books about time-out, get the tools ready, practice it in her head, and, the first time she can use it, freeze up and revert back to old, negative parenting patterns. Suddenly she'll find herself yelling, spanking, and getting frustrated.

Time-out is not complex. All it takes is willingness, a little preparation, and consistent follow-through. You might get worried that time-out won't work so you abandon the technique before you start. *But it does work, as thousands of parents have experienced.*

The Chair

When Joan's daughter, Amy, was a baby, Aunt Sally bought her a gorgeous hand-painted chair for $300.

When Amy turned two years old, Joan started to use time-out. She put Amy's beautiful chair in the hallway and sat Amy down in it. Joan continued to use this particular chair for time-out for the next six months.

After a while, Amy not only hated her beautiful hand-painted chair but also decided that it should "live" in the hallway permanently. When Aunt Sally came over and asked Amy how she liked her chair, Amy let Aunt Sally know in no uncertain terms that she didn't like it at all!

The chair is one of your most important tools in using time-out at home, but be careful about which chair you choose, or you might just be banning your favorite chair to the hallway.

Although time-out can be used in many places (I'll talk about that later), with or without a chair, the chair at home becomes the focal point for your child. You don't want to say "Go to the time-out chair," without a specific reference. The child should know which is *his* time-out chair and where time-out will be carried out. This information leads to consistency, and (as I will continue to emphasize) children respond positively to consistent discipline.

This problem occurred for Alan. Every time he told his son to go to time-out, the boy would go to his bedroom and play. Alan had no idea how to use time-out. He thought it meant the child should go to his room, a common error many parents make. Alan's son soon looked forward to his time-outs, somewhat like an exhausted basketball player looks forward to his.

Here are some of the basics of the time-out chair. The time-out chair should be a *nondescript* chair. It should be *small,* so it can be moved easily, and must be accessible for a small child to climb in and out of. As your child grows, you can change the chair.

Let your child know that the time-out chair is a place where he can go to quiet down and think about the problem behavior. Try to keep the chair as *neutral* as possible. Place the chair in a quiet hallway or corner. It is important to put the chair someplace quiet, not facing a window, a television, or the child's room. Some people prefer to leave the chair in place all the time, but I think this creates a negative mind-set for the child. It implies that another instance of misbehavior is just a matter of time and the chair is sitting and waiting for him.

The chair should also not be moved by the child during a time-out. The parent needs to tell the child that the time-out chair is a special place to "cool off." Try not to create a negative view of the chair by saying "This is where you go when you are bad."

Some children will become stubborn and refuse to go to the time-out chair. This is the point when your stomach starts to turn. I have heard from panicked parents who, fearing the child would refuse, became so anxiety ridden prior to even attempting time-out that they stopped before they began. When this happens, don't panic or start yelling. I remember running around our house after my daughter, screaming "Time-out! Go to your chair! It's time-out!" She hid under her bed and refused to come out. First I had to get hold of myself. Then, I had to take action.

If this scenario happens, it is best to get hold of your child and firmly sit him down on the chair. If the child jumps up out of the chair, put him back down and hold him in the chair during the time-out. This is not easy, and the first instance of this may cause you a great deal of stress. That is what your child hopes will happen. But children, once they realize you mean business, will settle down. *Do not give up.*

It is important to tell children why they are being put in time-out when you place them on the chair. A small child might not have a clue as to what he did wrong. For instance, say to your child, "Johnny, you are in time-out for hitting Jordan" or "Susie, you are in time-out for not listening when I told you to go to bed."

Be *short* and as *specific* as possible with your reasons for giving a time-out. Do not go on and on with a long, detailed explanation. A long explanation will probably yield you a puzzled look. Also, do not analyze the behavior of your child.

One concerned mother asked her three-year-old boy, "Why did you push Casey? What did you really want from him? I think we should explore your reasons for hitting because it is not a good way to communicate." The child, totally perplexed, turned right around and pushed Casey again. A more verbal communication works better with an older child during a family meeting—an open forum where everyone can express feelings.

Swift, specific actions are the best way to alter misbehavior. Overtalking to small children goes right over their heads. Don't start talking to a child during a time-out. If the child talks while sitting in time-out, do not answer. If the child is older than four, reset the time for another two minutes if he talks. For a child older than six, set the timer for twice the child's age. For instance, if a child is six, add another six minutes. After this happens a few times, the child will get the point: no talking in time-out.

The Timer

My friend Sharon owns one shaped like a worm. Her friend Amy has one with bunny ears and a tail. Then there is the purist who owns a simple white one such as those that have graced kitchens for dozens of years. I, myself, have a small, neon red one that resembles an apple.

No matter what size, shape, or color you own, the *timer* will certainly become one of your best time-out tools. When little eyes spy that small hunk of wonder, they know it is time for serious action.

Your watch can be used when your timer is not available,

but the timer works best. Maybe it's that "ding" at the end of time-out that causes your child to sigh with relief and bolt from the time-out chair like an Olympic runner at the sound of the starting gun. One little toddler learned to count by watching the timer tick away. For whatever reason, the timer works. But remember that "ding" is a way to welcome children back, to let them start fresh.

The timer signifies seriousness. It is a physical entity that children can relate to. Your child will have no chance to argue with you about when time-out begins and ends because the timer will let everyone know. Use of the timer is a way to distance yourself from your child and the bad behavior. By taking the control of the disciplinary act out of your hands during the time-out period, you diffuse the conflict and help your child calm down.

At times when I was in a rotten mood and took out all my anger on my daughter, I set the timer and took a ten-minute time-out for myself. I told my daughter that I was taking a time-out and I couldn't talk to her. This let my child know that adults need to pull back and be quiet for a short period of time. Obviously, the timer will not always be with you when you are out, but do not hesitate to take it on weekend outings or family vacations.

When five-year-old Justin went to Hawaii with his parents, his mother brought her trusty timer. When Justin misbehaved, he was given a time-out. Very distressed, he protested: "Why is the timer here in Hawaii, Mommy? Isn't it on vacation, too?"

Once you have introduced your child to the timer, you will need to know how to use it properly. When you call "Time-out," set the timer to one minute for each year of your child's age. For instance, for a child who is five years old, set the timer for five minutes. For one who is three years old, set the timer for three minutes.

Since every child is different, you may have to adjust the time according to your child's temperament. Billy, an overactive, rambunctious five-year-old, can barely sit still for one minute, let alone five. Five minutes to Billy probably seems like hours, and he is destined to fail a five-minute time-out. You want to keep your child in time-out so he can calm down and understand that there are consequences to bad behavior. But in Billy's case, I recommend putting him in time-out for two to three minutes. That is enough time for him to get the point, yet not so much time that he will constantly fail at time-out.

Some young toddlers will get the point in one minute. A nine-year-old may need a full ten minutes or more in order to get the point. Whatever the age of your children, parents have to make them understand that the timer is the symbol for time-out to begin and for them to quiet down and start over.

Some children have trouble letting go of anger, and you may have to talk them through the process. My daughter fumed all through her time-outs. She could not "let it go," but she did sit until her time was up. After the time-out, she would stomp away in a rage. At first, I wanted to put her back in time-out, but I realized that it wouldn't change her temperament. What is important is that your child can start over when the time-out is done. Parents should not continue to talk to children about what they did and show anger or berate them. This will negate the purpose and benefit of the time-out. We should have already told them why they got a time-out. Now, they need a hug and a chance to show good behavior. Don't give your child guilt. Give him positive reinforcement—a chance to feel that he isn't so horrible for misbehaving that you don't forgive him. Your child needs your support.

The Place

As I have said, where your child takes time-out in your home is important. The place establishes a point of reference for your child. The place also signals that you mean business.

You can follow some simple commonsense rules for choosing the place.

- Do not give time-out in the child's bedroom, a playroom, or any place where there might be distractions such as toys and television.

- Do not choose a place by a window. Again, the location might offer too many interesting distractions.

- Always tell your child what the time-out is for: "Time-out for hitting."

- The place should be free of things for the child to look at or touch.

- Place the child in a corner or facing a blank wall.

- Usually, an empty hallway is the best choice for time-out.

- If you choose a hallway, make sure there is no foot traffic, such as other children walking back and forth. Remember, you want your child to experience enough boredom and discomfort that time-out becomes something to avoid. That is why the place to give time-out at home becomes such an important aspect of the time-out prescription.

- Never pick a spot such as the kitchen or bathroom, where a young child could get hold of something dangerous.

TIME-OUT RULES FOR YOUR CHILD

- No getting out of the chair
- No talking while in time-out
- No getting up until the timer goes off
- No kicking or screaming while in the chair
- No toys, blankets, or other items allowed in the chair
- No watching TV while in time-out

Quick Time-Out Checklist for Parents

In *Time-Out for Toddlers,* we created the bedside checklist. That simple list of behaviors, expanded here, will quickly remind you what to do when your child is crying and having a tantrum while in the time-out chair.

- ☐ Do not talk to your child.

- ☐ Do not even glance at your child.

- ☐ Do not talk with your spouse or anyone else about your child's behavior if she is within earshot.

- ☐ Avoid showing anger by raising your voice.

- ☐ Keep calm (if possible).

- ☐ Occupy yourself with another activity while monitoring your child.

- ☐ If you need to reset the timer, do so quickly and quietly.

CHAPTER 3

The Time-Out Formula

When to Use Time-Out

Obedient children will sometimes naturally hop in the time-out chair, wait out their time, and go on their way as happy as can be. Then there are those I call the *time-out testers, wall-kickers,* and *hystericals.*

Time-out testers will defy you to put them in time-out. Once there, they make their and your time-out quite miserable. This type of child is usually temperamentally difficult and noncompliant. With a time-out tester, time-out may have to be a prelude to a further punishment.

Then there are the wall-kickers, who will do just that. They'll sit in the chair and kick the paint off of your wall until you give them attention or resign yourself to a chipped wall. This is what they want. For wall-kickers, I suggest placing the chair far away from any walls, furniture, or doors. If your child is a wall-kicker, tell her she can kick the air if she pleases, but if she kicks the walls, she will get double time on the timer. If she still insists, ground her and take away a privilege.

Hysteric children act as if you are being abusive when you put them in time-out. The drama starts to escalate as soon as they are told to go to the time-out chair. They'll sometimes hang onto your leg. They'll cry, whine, plead, and then usually escalate to near-hysteria to avoid punishment. This form of manipulation can break down a nervous, harried parent, especially when the parent is trying to put the child in time-out outside the home. You will feel like jumping in a hole when the child starts to scream. But you must prevail. If you show your child that you refuse to break down, she will see that you are not going to give in. Although this is not an easy task, usually all you need is *one* time to prove that you are in control.

Remember, these are the testers. Children will push the limits to see how far they can get. Time-out testers will push harder and further than most children, especially if you let them.

Boundaries and Limits

The big *B* word—*boundaries*—will be the core to disciplining a child. Our overall goal should be for our children to respect the limits we set and to know when they've gone too far. If you want discipline to be effective, you don't want to overuse time-out. Children can begin to feel that the slightest thing they do wrong will put them in the time-out chair. By the time this happens, the parent is totally frustrated, and the child is out of control. Many parents feel giving in is easier than enforcing limits. A child will detect this and push past you. You are actually creating an anxious child when you are too permissive. Children *want* boundaries, which give them a feeling of security.

Boundaries are *child* laws. Just as adults have laws of right and wrong to follow, boundaries are the laws of right and wrong that parents set up for a child. Most laws are created to keep people safe and from hurting one another or themselves. Think of "child laws" as utilizing the same basic concept. Most children will understand what a boundary is by age three. At that age children feel separate from their parents. They start to clearly understand the concept of yes and no.

Children who think they can push past boundaries, will, so it is up to you to follow these simple rules:

• Set limits early on.

• Be clear about what is expected of your child. For instance, when you say "Time to stop playing," let your child know she has some leeway—like giving extra time for cleanup. You can set the timer for ten to twenty minutes and say "When the timer goes off, you should have finished cleaning up."

- Follow through with time-out. Don't give idle threats and warnings, because eventually your child will disregard what you say.
- Be consistent.
- Use time-out immediately when your child does not comply with your requests.
- Never engage in a shouting match or argue. Walk away.

These simple rules, followed, can make your life much easier and help your child feel better too.

Working Through a Problem

We often assume that children know certain things intuitively and should be able to work things out by themselves. But young children often do not have the ability to problem-solve unless they are taught.

By teaching children to think through a problem, you help them to build self-esteem. Instead of giving them everything they ask for, you can encourage them to be resourceful. This type of encouragement will also stimulate creativity.

This is exemplified by Rena, a precocious seven-year-old. Rena loved the turkey sandwiches that her friend Alex's mom packed in her lunch. Rena would toss her own sandwiches in the trash. Finally, one day she decided to keep her sandwiches, sell them with lemonade on Saturdays, and pay her friend a nickel a day to bring an extra turkey sandwich for her.

Although Rena's mom objected to her paying Alex for the sandwiches and selling her own, she admired Rena's ingenuity and carefully planned-out program. This sort of independent problem solving will serve your child well as an adult. But as a child, the behavior may be inappropriate. You can help your child assess his actions. By doing so, your child learns to set his own internal limits.

The Spanking Rule

Spanking is a delicate subject that is difficult to broach with parents because it brings up a lot of emotions related to one's own childhood experiences. Most of the hundreds of parents I spoke to were spanked as children. Often their parents didn't have the knowledge and access to books, television, and seminars that advocate alternative discipline methods that parents have today. Only one woman I talked with told me her parents did not spank her as a child. "I thought my parents didn't care about me, because all of my friends got spanked. I wondered why I was being ignored." As a result, she would act out, hoping her parents would spank her or react to her.

My personal feeling is *do not spank your child*. If you do, you *are* giving the message that it is okay to hit. Your child will emulate your actions. Hitting can lead to violent behavior.

It is too easy to spank a child when you get angry. I have been there. When my daughter was a toddler, she ran across the street. I became frightened at first, and then furious. I spanked her little bottom, all the while thinking "I'm teaching her a lesson." Then I went into my room and cried.

Spanking my child was clearly not the answer. I felt that not only did I *not* make my point but she also was too young to understand why she was getting spanked. This is when I turned to time-out. I knew there had to be a more effective way to get through to a child than to hurt and frighten her.

Parents that use spanking will find it too easy to slap or hit a child. It is better to consistently use alternative discipline methods that do not damage a child's self-esteem and are not physically painful. Children want to please us. Don't alienate them by spanking.

I have previously suggested a swift, small swat on the behind if a child gets out of the time-out chair. But after trying this with my own child and talking with other parents, I found that a spanking only escalated the situation and made the child angrier and the parent more tense. This is not what time-out is trying to achieve. You want to diffuse a negative situation, not charge it up.

If you are using time-out because you want to teach your child that hitting is inappropriate, then how do you justify a spanking? You can't say "My hitting is different than yours." It's not. Hitting is a violent act, and spanking is hitting.

Alternatives to spanking are available if you need additional methods. Certainly the Positive Points Chart and removal of privileges (discussed in Chapters 4 and 6) are both highly effective with young children. When I tell my nine-year-old daughter that she won't be allowed to go to her friend's birthday party if she does not do her homework, her little legs carry her to her desk *very* fast.

If you do ever spank your child in a fit of anger, say that you are sorry, that you acted inappropriately, and that hitting is not OK.

Count to Ten

Giving children a chance to behave is a better approach to parenting than shouting them down without warning. Some children, especially temperamentally difficult ones, can have trouble listening and/or doing what you ask immediately. Children will test a limit if they don't want to stop what they are doing. The Count to Ten Rule is a prelude to time-out. Counting to ten gives your child time to "get it together." She knows that on the count of ten you mean business—you will follow through with time-out.

Let's say you want your child to turn off the television and get ready for bed. You make the request, but it falls on deaf ears. You ask again, but your child still doesn't listen. Finally, you scream. The child gets upset, you're upset, and not much is accomplished.

It is much simpler to say "You have until the count of ten to turn off the television and get into bed." Then, without any further discussion, start counting. A child will usually hesitate until the count of three, but by five the TV is off and the child is jumping into bed. By ten, the light is off.

This technique is highly effective. Perhaps the structure and challenge of the ten-count is what stimulates the child into action. If by the count of ten the child has not complied with your request, back it up with a time-out. You can give a time-out before bed because it often will quiet a child down.

The Count to Ten Rule keeps you in control. But remember these simple rules when counting to ten:

- Don't threaten to use it. Use it!

- Use it after no more than two requests.

- No parental whining, "Why don't you ever listen?"

- Don't wait for a time-out after ten.

- No double counting. Don't say "I'll give you one more ten-count." *Ten is ten.*

Consistency

Consistency! Consistency! This word should become your discipline mantra. Many parents have learned the hard way that once they stop being consistent, children stop listening. The child thinks "Since mom didn't put me in time-out last time because I whined, maybe she won't this time."

Parents may think that once a behavior is corrected, they can ease up with time-out. Chances are, they will undo all their good work, and the problem will return.

You need to consistently back up what you say with *action.* Otherwise, your words have little impact on your child. Consistency is like a boundary. It is a way of keeping our children on target and safe. Otherwise, they will constantly be testing to see if they can get away with something.

Use time-out every time your child misbehaves. Don't let anything deter your disciplinary action. If you are in a public place or with other people, use time-out. By responding consistently, you are giving your child the message "I am in control. I want to help you act appropriately because I love you. I will put you on time-out." A child who knows that you mean business will be less likely to misbehave.

Consistency on your part will eventually lead to consistent behavior on your child's part.

The time-out formula incorporates three important things: boundaries and limits, counting to ten, and consistency. By using this triad with time-out, you are building your parental discipline tools. You will be empowered because you will have discipline choices when your child misbehaves. You will be better able to implement time-out and probably have to use it less frequently.

Time-Out Checklist

- ☐ Do not talk to a child who is on time-out.

- ☐ Do not yell.

- ☐ Do not threaten without backup. If you say you are going to put your child on time-out, do it.

- ☐ Do not wait until your child is out of control and seriously misbehaving. Use time-out often.

- ☐ Place the chair facing a boring wall or in a hallway.

- ☐ Make sure there are no distractions—television, other children playing, toys to look at, a window view.

CHAPTER 4

Positive Reinforcement

Separating the Child from the Behavior

"You are terrible. I can't stand you!" That's what a friend of
mine remembered her mother saying to her once, only once,
when she was a child. It made a lasting impression on my
friend. She said, "I never quite felt the same about myself
after that. I always wondered if she meant it."

We are not all easygoing and patient parents. Sometimes
our children drive us crazy. They can hit unbelievably sensitive buttons. It is not uncommon to snap at a child when we
are in a foul mood or when that child pushes too far. The
key is remembering not to tell our children they are bad or
that we don't like them.

Always separate the child's behavior from the child. Our
children need to understand that their behavior is bad—not
them. Make this very clear. Here are some appropriate
responses to a child's misbehavior:

- "Your *behavior* is not acceptable."
- "The way you acted is inappropriate."
- "It is not OK to hit."

Conversely, negative statements such as, "I don't like you," "You are a bad boy," and "You're obnoxious" can devastate a child's fragile ego. He can start to believe he is not likable and act out in inappropriate ways. Psychologically, the child may think, "If my parents think I'm not likable, then I must not be, so why bother to be good—to listen. No matter what I do, it won't matter." This is all subliminal thought, but children take what we say literally. They believe what we tell them. That is why we must think about what messages we want to give our children—what we want to teach them. A child will model and react to whatever a parent does.

Joyce was furious with her friend. They were having a heated disagreement over the phone. Her five-year-old son, Josh, was sitting in the next room. The following day, Josh was playing with his friend. Josh wanted his toy back, but his friend did not want to oblige. Josh yelled, "Give me my goddamn toy back." Joyce came running in from the other room, mouth agape. "Josh, you're disgusting. Where did you learn that language?"

"I learned it from you, Mommy." Indeed he did. Not that every child will pick up and use everything you say, but precocious children will parrot what they hear, often with proper usage. Certainly such children cannot be blamed for what they say.

It is up to the parent to discuss appropriate and inappropriate responses to situations. A time-out is called for when a child is clearly old enough to know the difference between right and wrong. But before snapping at a child, try to separate a response that seems out of character for him. If you have discussed what is not acceptable in your household and the child uses bad language, then use time-out.

Children are not bad. Often they have no idea what they are saying. Find the source for your child's behavior first, before you react.

Mirroring

Mirroring is an excellent technique for helping your child express feelings. It prevents you, the parent, from getting pulled into a negative interaction. Mirroring lets you mirror back your child's anger and diffuse it by not engaging in further oppositional dialogue.

For instance, seven-year-old Evan was furious at his school coach. He went out for the football team, and his friend made the team, but Evan didn't. He got so angry that he threw the football over the fence into the street. He got into trouble for throwing the football and had to go to the principal's office. When he returned from school, his mother was able to mirror him by saying, "You must be very angry and disappointed that you didn't make the team, but it is still not OK to act out when you are angry." Mom can offer other alternatives for his anger.

Mirroring helps you to stay away from negative phrasing that disregards your child's feelings, such as "You shouldn't feel that way," "Don't get so angry," and "Don't make a big deal out of it." Let your child talk and be angry. Acknowledge the anger. If you don't, he will feel more frustrated. Offer him a punching bag, a place to "scream out" that anger, and a shoulder to cry on.

Fairness

It is important that you have a fair and realistic view of your child and discipline. You need to carefully assess your motivations when you discipline and make sure you are being fair. Often, what is normal behavior for a child can grate on a parent's nerves and cause the parent to be too harsh on the child.

There are many ways to avoid time-out if you are willing to take some responsibility for your actions and mood. By not jumping on your child too often and using other alternative methods of negotiation, the use of time-out, when appropriate, will have a greater impact.

You can unintentionally expect too much from your child. Therefore, if you ask your child to do a task, it can become a power struggle. There are a number of ways to teach your child to be independent without yelling or arguing.

For instance, five-year-old Laura constantly argued with her mother, Janet, about getting dressed. Laura wanted her mom to dress her. Janet felt Laura was old enough to dress herself. They would get into power struggles. Laura refused to get dressed, so Janet would give in and dress her, but she became angry at Laura for manipulating her.

If Janet wanted to teach Laura to get dressed herself, she needed ways to problem-solve through the task, thus encouraging Laura's independence, but doing so in a positive manner.

Don't Argue

When your child argues with everything you say, it is best to pull back and join his thoughts. If you have a toddler, it is best to redirect his thinking by getting him involved in a different activity. Some children live for power struggles, but if you agree with your child or present alternatives, there is nothing to argue about.

This is exemplified by Amy, who fought with her daughter Tara about practicing the piano. Tara simply refused, even though she was the one who begged for lessons. Amy gave up the constant fighting and simply told the piano teacher not to come. Tara was so upset on the day of her lesson that she sat for an hour waiting for her teacher. Amy simply told Tara, "Since you didn't want to practice, I realized you didn't really want lessons, so I canceled them."

Tara started to cry. She told her mom that she did *want* lessons and that she would practice from now on.

Offer Choices

Parents can become like dictators. At some point, the monarchy (child) rebels, and then comes the war. A child should, if the situation is appropriate, be given choices in areas of dress, foods, friends, and toys. The parent has the responsibility to see that the initial choices are OK. The parent needs to determine moral and safety factors. By giving choices, you will have less manipulating and temper flare-ups.

By giving choices, you teach your child to eventually learn to make appropriate choices on his own. But not every situation is negotiable. If you decide that the decision is yours alone, let your child know that the choice is not his to make and then end the discussion.

Blame

When anything went wrong in Blair's house, she immediately blamed her precocious little boy, Paul. Paul was always getting in trouble, and Blair was preconditioned to react the minute anything went wrong. Paul's sister, Mia, was the perfect child. She never seemed to get into trouble and was compliant with her mother's requests.

When a glass plate broke, Blair immediately blamed Paul and sent him to time-out without an explanation. Paul got hysterical. He said it wasn't his fault, but Blair saw him next to the plate and blamed him. What really happened was that

Mia was playing with the plate. Paul was standing there watching her. The plate fell and broke, and Mia ran off. Paul started to play with the broken pieces and his mother saw him. Blair immediately reacted. She was conditioned to blame Paul.

In order to avoid unfair blame on your child, you need to approach each situation with compassion:

- Assume your child is innocent until proven otherwise.
- Don't play favorites.
- Some things are accidents. Let your child have a chance to tell you what happened.

Just as you would teach the concept of fair play with other children, you need to be fair with your child. A parent can be reactive and punish a child needlessly.

Laugh with Me

Parents often forget how to laugh with their children. We can get into such a negative cycle of disciplining our children all the time that we forget how to enjoy them. We might overlook their good qualities—curiosity, humor, and exuberance. And humor can diffuse a potentially explosive situation.

Catch your child off-guard sometime. Let him see that you are not just a "time-out machine" that never likes to have any fun and waits for him to disobey so you can get angry.

Children sometimes cease to see parents as humans. You become the enemy. It is better to be a friend.

My husband, who can be a stern disciplinarian, was having dinner with our daughter at a casual hamburger restaurant. She started whining and getting cranky. Instead of snapping at her or threatening a time-out, he threw some French fries at her. She was stunned and started to giggle. She threw one back at him. This went on for a few minutes until both "children" settled down. My daughter was so delighted to see her dad in this new way. It was worth the catsup-smeared T-shirts. All of a sudden he seemed more human to her: he had a sense of humor. I really think this incident positively changed their relationship from then on. She became less obstinate; he became less stern. They found a happier medium in the parent-child relationship.

A child can become defensive, thinking the parent represents negative interaction. If you engage your child in some friendly and fun time, he will view you differently. This does not mean you have to give up your rules or standards. Just approach a situation with less venom and more humor. It creates a more positive and loving interaction between you and your child.

Positive "Strokes"

No doubt you have heard about using positive reinforcement with your child. I cannot overstate how important positive strokes are, but we need to clarify the difference between positive strokes and overpraise. Some parents spend so much time overpraising everything the child does that the impact is lost. Giving positive strokes for positive behavior is important. You want your child to have good self-esteem. This should be your primary goal in parenting. Self-esteem is tied not to how many toys or material objects children have but to how they feel about themselves. Positive reinforcement can help children view themselves as worthwhile, by giving them the message "You're terrific. What you say and do is worthwhile. You count!" After a while a child will transfer positive strokes onto himself and give himself the message "I'm terrific. I care for myself."

When children view themselves positively, it is easier to get them to follow rules and start behaviors that we want accomplished, like making the bed, doing homework, and brushing teeth. Seeing themselves as good people, they want to please so they can receive more positive strokes.

Giving positive praise to your child for little successes is important, but you don't want to become obsessive about it. Overpraise can create unrealistic expectations in a child. If we praise children for everything they do, from eating their vegetables to going to sleep, they will *expect* praise constantly. If they don't get it, they wonder why.

Underpraise

Just as overpraise can be nonconstructive, underpraising your child can hurt a young child's fragile ego. Most parents teach their children the simple adage, "If you can't say anything nice, don't say anything at all." These words of wisdom should apply to parents as well.

A parent's words can have a strong impact on a child. If you constantly underpraise and look for the negative in your child's behavior, then he will act out your expectations or become tentative and frightened. A child will begin to see himself in a negative light. It is vital that a child sees himself as capable, confident, and acceptable. Your overall goal should be to help your child build his own self-esteem and view himself in a positive light. A child needs to make mistakes so he can learn, grow, and correct himself.

One impatient father never let his son pour his own milk. Even when the boy turned seven years old, Dad still was pouring his milk. When the boy attempted to pour, his father said, "I'll do it. You'll just spill it." The boy felt no sense of independence. And when his father constantly demeaned or underpraised the small things he tried to do, the boy felt disempowered.

So what if he spills the milk. We have to be willing to let our children make mistakes. That is how children learn. Of course, we don't let them do anything dangerous. Assess the task according to the child's age and let him try new things with your guidance.

Encourage independent behavior with gentle help. Give positive strokes when your child completes a task or even attempts it. A typical task for a three-year-old might be saying "thank you" or playing nicely with a friend. For a seven-year-old, an appropriate task might be getting a good grade on an important school project, sharing with a sibling, or using good manners with new friends and relatives.

We need not continually praise a task that our children are expected to complete on a daily basis. Give positive strokes to reinforce good behavior, but don't overpraise children for every small thing they do. And don't underpraise them when they try their best to accomplish a new task.

Charting Your Child's Progress

In conjunction with time-out, a Positive Points Chart is a good reinforcer to use with your child. A simple chart can help motivate even the most uncooperative child into action. What's important in the beginning is to tie the points to a nonmaterial reward. Eventually, the child will not need the chart because the behavior will become rote—instinctive. The chart will motivate him. Once he receives continued positive reinforcement for good behavior, the reinforcement itself will be the reward.

Some children who are temperamentally difficult will respond well to a Positive Points Chart. It sets up a structure proved by child psychologists to be helpful with challenging children. But all children can benefit from a structured discipline that rewards good behavior. It is another way to prompt self-esteem in your child by reinforcing positive behavior.

You can fill in the points chart with whatever behaviors

you feel are important and you want to work on. You should list things that are age-appropriate for your child. You wouldn't put, "Make your bed" in the chart for a three-year-old, but you might want to encourage positive behavior by giving points when your child reverses a negative behavior. For instance, your child grabs his sister's toys on a day-to-day basis. Let's say you want to encourage positive behavior and behavioral changes by saying "I will give you a point if you *don't* grab your sister's toys."

Make new charts as the child grows, and you want to encourage or correct behaviors. By using charts, we put the children in charge of their behavior, and we are no longer the "bad guy." They have to take responsibility for their good or bad behavior. We are just there to cheer them on.

During the course of a day, every time your child displays one of the positive behaviors that you have charted, give him a point. For a younger child, use stars or hearts or happy faces. Be your child's advocate. Express a lot of praise when he earns positive points.

For a younger child, you can add up the points at the end of the day and give a small reward along with a lot of praise. For an older child, you might want to add up the points at the end of the week and give a reward such as a sleepover, a movie, or getting to stay up an hour longer at night.

Remember, the points earned should have intrinsic rewards, so don't give any elaborate rewards such as expensive toys. You are trying to both change behavior and create internal motivation.

If your child does have a bad day, don't penalize him. Continue to encourage good behavior. Let him know he "can do it." Also, do not set the points so high that it will be impossible for him to attain the goal. For instance, if fourteen points are possible at the end of the week, don't hold back a reward if your child only has thirteen. Try to reward each step of the way.

If your child misbehaves, use time-out. Do not take points away. By taking points away, you are sending mixed signals—one minute you are praising the good behavior, and the next minute you are taking away the praise. Always separate positive-points behavior from any negative, time-out behaviors.

You should use the positive points until your child's behavior changes. Once the behavior improves, continue to reinforce the good behavior with lots of verbal praise.

If you find the behavior is not changing, ask yourself these questions:

- ◆ Are you praising the positive behavior?
- ◆ Did you forget to give points?
- ◆ Are you using time-out for misbehavior?
- ◆ Are you being consistent?
- ◆ Did you and your child discuss how the chart works and what the rewards are?
- ◆ Is the reward appropriate for the behavior?

Use the sample points charts to set up your child's chart.

POSITIVE POINTS CHART
For Preschool Child

Task	Sunday	Monday	Tuesday	Wednesday	Thursday	Friday	Saturday
Brush teeth							
Help make bed							
Pick up toys							
Do homework							
Feed dog			★				★
Use please and thank-you							

POSITIVE POINTS CHART
For Six- to Ten-Year-Old

Task	Sunday	Monday	Tuesday	Wednesday	Thursday	Friday	Saturday
Make bed							
Brush teeth							
Do homework							
Clean hamster cage			✓				✓
Set the table							

CHAPTER 5

Communicate with Care

Communication is the key to all aspects of getting your child to behave. Both verbal and nonverbal communication can be a source for effective discipline. You can communicate what you want from your child by good role-modeling, clear rule setting, and agreement between caregivers.

Parents need to be in sync as to how they will talk to and discipline their child. If mom yells but dad says time-out and mom disagrees, then chances are the child will be confused. Both parents and caregivers need to know what behaviors get a time-out, what "language" is OK or not OK. If your home is going to be run like a democracy, then make sure everyone gets a vote. If not, establish who is in charge.

Family meetings are an excellent forum for communication because they are based on cooperation and not on attack. Once a week, sit down as a family and discuss problems as honestly as possible without hurting feelings. Each person should be allowed to speak without interruption for approximately five minutes. During your meetings, discuss rules with your child and what is acceptable and unacceptable.

Effective Nonverbal Communication

The way you communicate nonverbally to your child is as important as your verbal communication. Also, by using nonverbal communication, you can catch your child off-guard. If he is always expecting a lecture or a yelling parent, the signals you give him can say more than you realize.

I know a parent who only has to raise one eyebrow and her children know immediately that "mom means business." Another simply taps twice with his foot; the kids know that if Dad taps three times, they are in deep trouble.

Nonverbal communication can be used to convey many types of messages to your child. A pat on the back or stroke of the cheek tells your child that she is loved and appreciated. If you give this type of touch when your child is playing nicely, then you are nonverbally saying, "I like that you are playing so nicely and sharing your toys." A high-five after a soccer game tells your child that he was great (whether his team won or lost).

A hug, a kiss, a smile can say volumes to a child in need of encouragement. Conversely, if you want to show disapproval of your child's actions, you can communicate your intentions by

- ◆ Making eye contact
- ◆ Having a serious expression

- Facing your child toward you (sitting or kneeling at his level)
- Not speaking unless you know you have his attention

Nonverbal communication is a powerful way to let your child know how you feel without raising your voice. It can also be a strong way to express positive and loving feelings.

Respecting the Rules

Communicating respect is not something you can demand from a child. But you can instill it by example. One of the rules of seven-year-old Becky's house was "No eating in the bedroom." When Becky's friend, Lauren, came for a play date, Lauren took her snack into Becky's room. Becky told Lauren, "We can't eat in the bedrooms." But Lauren said, "Your mom is eating in her bedroom. Why can't we?"

Clearly miffed at Mom, Becky asked her, "Why can you eat in your room, but I can't?" Mom was at a loss for words and quickly took her coffee and crackers to the kitchen.

A lot of conflict can be avoided if you are *very* clear about the rules of your home. If you are respectful of the rules, your children will be, too. If you follow rules, so will your child. Instill pride in your home and things. Set a good example. If you have separate rules for the adults in your home, then discuss them and make it clear that adults follow different rules than children do. Expect some "whys." Make a rules chart and go over them with your child.

We can encourage our children to remind their friends

about the rules of the house. They can tell friends that they get a time-out for breaking the house rules. Encourage children to make up some of the rules. Let them have a part in writing down and discussing rules.

The illustration of Respecting-the-Rules Chart will give you an idea of how a rules chart could be set up. There is no set way to do one. What's important is that the family do it together.

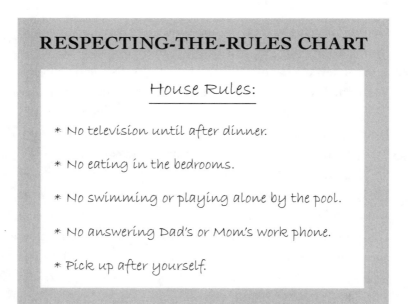

RESPECTING-THE-RULES CHART

House Rules:

* No television until after dinner.

* No eating in the bedrooms.

* No swimming or playing alone by the pool.

* No answering Dad's or Mom's work phone.

* Pick up after yourself.

Natural Consequences

Do you ever feel as if you are talking to your child but no one is home in that little head? You may have asked or requested the same thing a hundred times, but your child won't listen. Perhaps the only way to get through to some children is to hope natural consequences take effect.

Eight-year-old Rebecca refused to take regular baths. Her mother, Annie, would argue, yell, and put her on time-out, but bath time became a nightmare. Annie finally decided to let Rebecca stay dirty and hope consequences came out of it. Her plan worked. Some of Rebecca's friends remarked that she was "stinky." After tears and hurt feelings, Rebecca decided to take more showers because "I'm not stinky!"

Letting our children get their feelings hurt or get in trouble with their teacher is not easy. But with some children, not until we let them pay the consequences for their own contrary actions or behavior will our repeated requests sink into their heads. If your child whines and refuses when asked to take a sweater, what is the natural consequence? Instead of getting into an argument, let him go without one. If the day is chilly, he will feel the bite of the cold—and listen the next time you suggest a sweater. *Suggest* is the word I use, because suggest is what you should do. If you demand or cajole, your child will end up being stubborn and noncompliant. Make your request *once*, firmly, and then let it go.

The rules about natural consequences are:

- Never allow your child to play with or attempt anything dangerous.

- Certain rules of the house are not negotiable.

- Don't say "I told you so" to your child.

- Don't allow your child to hurt or embarrass anyone else by his actions.

Talking Effectively

Talking to children can be much more challenging than talking to an adult. We parents often either patronize our children or speak way over their heads. Also, children will tune us out if they think we don't mean business. To communicate effectively, so your child will listen, you must learn to talk in an assertive manner. Often parents, frustrated by their inability to evoke a desired behavior, get into an angry mode with children. But children do not understand the innuendoes, subtleties, and idioms of language. We need to speak on their level, not expect them to come up to ours. I have often heard parents yelling at a child, "What's wrong with you? Don't you understand what I'm saying?" In truth, the child may not understand what we parents are saying.

To talk effectively, make sure you have made eye contact with your child. Be clear. Do not use language that your child does not understand.

When "No" Means Yes

Five-year-old Andrew wanted a doughnut. His mother, Judy, said, "No. It's too close to dinnertime."

Andrew started to whine, "But I'm so hungry!"

Judy said, "No!"

Andrew pleaded, "Can I just have half?"

Judy replied, "No. Don't you listen?"

Andrew responded, "Please, Mommy. I love sprinkle doughnuts. Please!"

Judy answered, "Andrew, I said no! Why don't you hear what I'm telling you?"

"Please, please, please," whined Andrew. "I'm *so* hungry."

Judy: "All right, just a half and that's it. Do you hear me?"

Judy said no, but Andrew got his doughnut. The lines of communication definitely did not work out as planned. Andrew knows that, if he negotiates, whines, and coerces his mom, eventually he'll get what he wants. If the boundary of "no" is not established early on, a child will keep pushing until he gets what he wants. A lot of time-outs can be avoided if you say what you mean and follow through.

What happens to a parent who allows the child to push past parental limits is *anger.* The parent is angry at himself for giving in to the child and takes out his anger on the child. Judy was furious when Andrew didn't want to eat his dinner. She yelled at Andrew, "See what happens when you eat sweets before dinner?"

Learning to talk to your child isn't as easy as it sounds. Avoiding empty threats is vital. Some of the following points will help you communicate more effectively with your child and give you an idea of what not to do.

- Threatening a time-out will probably not get a child to behave if you wait and don't follow through.
- Avoid asking silly questions. Don't ask a young child why

he is throwing his food or not listening. Chances are you'll get a silly answer or no answer at all.

- "I'm begging you." Never show your vulnerable side to your child by trying to cajole him into obeying you.

- Don't ignore the problem. It won't go away. I promise. Deal with it directly.

- A put-down sets up your child to be angry and verbally abusive back to you. Never swear or use derogatory language toward your child.

- "Large" threats, such as threatening to take summer camp away or trying to frighten your child into submissive behavior, won't work. A child will learn to disregard such threats.

- If you display physically abusive or screaming behavior, your child will emulate you. Your goal is to get your child to stay in control. Having an adult temper tantrum is inappropriate role modeling.

There are effective ways to get through to your child. Some of the following suggestions on the Parent Assertive Checklist will help you stay in control and better communicate with your child.

Parent Assertive Checklist

- ☐ *Be clear.* State what you want in a simple and concise manner.

- ☐ Do not use statements such as "Maybe," "We'll see,"

"Perhaps," "Well, I'm not sure," "I'll think about it," or "You'd better, or else!"

☐ When you speak, look into your child's eyes. Make sure he has eye contact with you.

☐ Think about the misbehavior before you administer the punishment. You might be impulsive and give too harsh a punishment.

☐ *Listen.* Sometimes you need to hear your child's side of the story. You can say "I hear what you have to say. But I am the parent, and you need to take a time-out."

☐ Don't ask: "Would you like to set the table now?" "How about cleaning up your room?" If you ask rather than tell your child what you want, you're in for trouble. Tell.

CHAPTER 6

Time-Out
Variables

Getting Feelings Out

Sometimes you may think something is wrong with your child. Yet, you fail to examine changes in the child's life.

Think about how stress can affect you: nervous stomach, sleeplessness, tension, headaches. Children may react to stress in different ways. They might act out, throw things, refuse to go to bed, or not eat properly. Before you send your child to the time-out chair, ask yourself some questions:

- Are there any changes in your household?
- Is there a new baby in the house?
- Is someone ill?
- Are you and your spouse arguing?
- Are you moving?
- Is your child having problems in school?

Children need emotional outlets. They are not always misbehaving when they act out feelings. If there is a valid reason for your child's misbehavior, then you might need to give her room to get her feelings out. Make your child aware that you know some changes are going on. Acknowledge her feelings: "I know you might be nervous about this move, and I understand your feelings."

Don't tell your child that she shouldn't feel the way she does. You might be moving to a fabulous new house on a block full of kids, but that doesn't discount her nervousness about her new surroundings. Try to ease your child into a new situation.

Children will almost surely act out when a new sibling arrives. Remember, your child has been the center of attention, and you have the nerve to bring home a new baby who is taking a lot of that attention. Give your child extra attention when a new baby arrives. Such children might even regress and want to be babied, too. Toddlers will usually want to nurse or want a bottle and more cuddle time with mommy and daddy. Indulge such feelings for a while. Then stress the importance of being a big brother or sister to the new baby and guide your toddler through the process of holding and loving the new sibling.

Parental Feelings

There is nothing as painful as seeing your child's feelings get hurt. When Shirley's daughter, Jill, was left out of a party with a group of girls, Shirley felt angry and hurt for her daughter. Shirley acted out her own anger, which only made Jill more anxious and upset. Now Jill was dealing with her mother's feelings as well as her own. Jill needed someone to identify and acknowledge *her* feelings.

A child wants a parent to listen and be there—not to partner her feelings. It becomes too emotionally overwhelming, especially for a small child, to witness a parent's angry outburst.

The following is a list of statements that can be used in various social situations that may arise with your child. As discussed in Chapter 4, you can help your child mirror her feelings by reflecting back your thoughts in a more constructive and positive way.

Inappropriate Responses	Appropriate Parental Responses
I hate Kathy for not inviting me.	You must be angry at Kathy because she didn't invite you to the party.
I never want to play with her again.	You might want to think about your friendship and how important it is to you.
I'm never going to invite her to my party.	Wait until you calm down and then decide who you want to invite.

Encourage your child to talk out her feelings, not only with you but with the child she is angry at. You will empower your child when you teach her how to talk to people in a nonconfrontational way. But you must model this same type of behavior for her.

Always engage your child in conversation. Allow her to express feelings without being censored. If things are said that you disapprove of, discuss calmly why the words, not the feelings, are inappropriate. Children will often use language to catch a parent off-guard. If a child continues to act out over a new situation, explain what the consequences are if the behavior continues.

Ask a lot of questions and truly be interested in your child's life, but when she says she doesn't want to tell you any more, don't take it personally. We need to allow our children privacy but let them know that we are always available to talk.

Double Trouble: Time-Out for Two Kids

The thought of putting two children on time-out might leave you in a panic, but this can be done effectively. Often, when two children are fighting, determining who is at fault is hard.

Johnny screams, "Susie hit me!" Susie yells back, "He hit me first." Johnny insists, "No, I didn't." Susie cries, "Liar, liar."

By this time, you are either playing referee or yelling like a crazy person, or both. For this reason, it is best to put both children on a time-out for cooldown. Of course, as a parent, you will need to assess what occurred and decide whether one child is *clearly* at fault. However, experience dictates that it usually does "take two" to create a confrontation.

The key to double time-out is that you want to avoid having two children in close proximity, giggling and making funny faces at one another. Put the two children on time-out in two different rooms or two different corners with their backs to one another. Any giggling, talking, or turning around will get both of them more time on the timer.

If you are not at home, you can use the same "time-out anywhere" technique, but you will probably need to stand between the two children so you don't lose sight of them or let them get out of control.

You can combine double time-out with removal of privileges and any other methods that you have found effective with two children. Sometimes, you may have to experiment to see what your children respond to most. But time-out should always be used as a way to quickly diffuse conflict. Two screaming children need a way to stop escalating anger before it gets out of control.

Someone Else's Child

When the second child is someone else's, parents can have mixed feelings about using time-out; disciplining someone else's child is uncomfortable. However, if a child is totally misbehaving in your home, it may be necessary. Clearly, you need to discuss this with the parent of your child's friend.

Breaking up a fight between friends can be difficult. For one reason, you don't want to yell at someone else's child. On the other hand, to discipline your child alone may not be fair if she wasn't at fault or the friend was causing problems. With elementary school children, the best thing to do is to say "Time-out for cool-off." Send each child into a different room for a short period of time. Then let them come back, shake hands, and start fresh. Most parents will actually appreciate this way of handling conflict.

Siblings

Sibling rivalry will always exist. It is the nature of siblings to compete for parents' time and attention. However, although yelling, teasing, and fighting can be normal for siblings, some parents can't tolerate this behavior. If we put our children on time-out every time they argue, they'll be sitting on those chairs all the time.

The key things to remember with siblings is fairness. If you hear fighting, make both children responsible. Don't go back and forth trying to find out who started the argument. Unless you are positive who started it, put *both* children on time-out. If you put both on time-out, both will think twice before acting out the next time. Here are some time-out guidelines:

- *Any* physical fighting will get a time-out.

- Each child should have her own time-out chair and corner, away from the other.

- Have siblings' meetings with each child. Encourage them to talk out their feelings and what bothers them. Have them (not you) find ways to solve it.

- Be their advocate, not their referee.

Removal of Privileges

Time-out is a great discipline tool. Along with time-out, however, other methods of discipline can be highly effective, especially for a strong-willed child. The threat of removal of privileges, better known as "grounding," can be a big incentive for a child to behave. What privilege you choose to remove will depend on the age and maturity of the child.

A child does not like to lose anything, especially a social plan. Although canceling a play date or sleepover is upsetting—for both children involved—it is ultimately your child's responsibility to explain why she could not play with her friend. Most other parents will understand your actions and even respect you for it. But do not worry about what another parent thinks of you. Every parent has a different method of disciplining a child. Once you have made a decision to take away a privilege (such as a play date), you should not be embarrassed or intimidated by other children or parents.

For a younger child, simply removing a toy or television privilege can make an impact. For an older child, you can remove a play date or Nintendo privileges.

Decide how severe the misbehavior is and discipline accordingly. Getting in a physical fight at school should warrant removal of privileges for one week or more. Talking back or not listening to you might justify no television for two nights. Try not to take away things such as sports. Your child is part of a team, and the discipline should not penalize an entire team of children. You have to clarify the rules of your family for your child and let her know what is acceptable and unacceptable behavior and what the consequences are—time-out, removal of privileges.

Time-out works most effectively for an immediate infraction that takes place while you are present. But for misbehaviors at school or somewhere else, a removal of privileges works well. A time-out after the fact will not have as strong an impact as "No TV tonight."

Time-Out Anywhere

Often your child doesn't think that you would dream of giving a time-out away from home. Don't even hesitate! Successful time-outs in other places can secure your time-out technique. If you follow through, your child will know you are serious and will think twice before testing your limits.

Time-outs in places outside the home can be tricky. Obviously you won't have all of your time-out tools with

RULES FOR REMOVAL
OF PRIVILEGES

1. Follow through. *Never* give a threat you don't plan to carry out.

2. Make sure the punishment fits the crime. For instance, don't take away a best friend's slumber party if your child forgets her sweater at school.

3. Use age-appropriate consequences.

4. Stay firm. When you remove a privilege, do not give it back if your child begs or pleads.

5. Don't punish yourself. Think through your choice of privilege removal *before* you do it. If you take away a sleepover and you and your husband were going out that night, then you have to stay home or hire a baby-sitter.

6. Do not worry about what the other child or parent will think if you take away a play date. Remind your child that her behavior caused the disciplinary action. She is responsible.

7. Do not remove a transitional object such as a beloved blanket or stuffed animal, if your child is a toddler. This will only cause undue anxiety for your child.

you, although I have been accused of taking my timer with me to Disneyland. My daughter, Alexandra, got a time-out on the edge of the Haunted Mansion next to Splash Mountain. If you aren't as compulsive as I am, you can use your watch or just count down the time.

When my daughter was four years old, we went to my cousin's wedding. During the ceremony, my little one wanted to run around and play with the flowers. Of course, this was not allowed, but she became persistent and loud.

I picked her up, took her outside, and put her on time-out in front of the hors d'oeuvres and cocktail table. She was shocked. She cried. She was embarrassed, especially since she had twenty nervous waiters staring at her. I was not thrilled that I had to miss part of the ceremony, but my cousin would never have forgiven me if I had allowed my daughter to ruin her wedding.

Time-out is not just reserved for your house. It is definitely a portable discipline technique. You'll just have to use your imagination sometimes. You don't want your child to think "I have to be good at home, but I can go crazy at other places because Mommy and Daddy don't have the chair, the timer, and the corner with them." The message you want your child to get is "I better behave because Mom and Dad will put me on time-out anywhere!"

Don't feel hesitant or embarrassed to use time-out away from your home. Otherwise, your child might act out and misbehave because she knows you are unwilling to discipline her. It will be better than yelling or spanking your child in public. Physical public discipline can scar a child emotionally; it is humiliating and embarrassing for the child. But time-out removes your child from other people and allows for a cool-down time.

Think of time-out as portable parenting. Here are some ideas on ways to handle a time-out in a variety of places.

- If you are in a car and you need to stop for time-out, pull off and either give time-out in the back of the car or have your child sit on a curb by the car while you stand next to her.

- If you are shopping in a department store, use a dressing room.

- In place of a chair, your child can sit on a bench, in a dressing room, or on the grass at a park, or just have her stand in a corner. You might have to get creative. At Disneyland, my daughter sat on a plastic log.

- If you are at a place of worship, go outside or to the bridal room.

- A restaurant is a child's favorite place to act out, usually at about the time when the food arrives. Take the child out of the restaurant and put her on time-out either in your car or in front of the restaurant in a quiet area away from people so you do not embarrass her.

- If you are alone and with more than one child, you may feel lost if you need to put one child on time-out and not leave the other. The best solution for this situation is to turn your child around, either in a chair or in a booth, cut the time-out in half, and do not speak to her until it is over.

Don't let the fact that you are in a public place deter you. That is exactly what your child is hoping for.

In some instances, time-outs can be extremely difficult. An airplane or movie theater is not an optimal place for time-outs. Yet, some creative parents have managed to put their children on time-out regardless of the venue. However, you might not feel as comfortable and may need some alternative discipline methods.

I feel time-out should be immediate. In some instances, however, time-out can wait until you get home. Particularly with older children, you can delay a time-out without having it lose its impact. For instance, if you are unable to give your six-year-old a time-out, say "You will get your time-out when we get home." The minute you walk in the door put your child on time-out. Obviously, delaying a time-out more than a few hours is not advisable, especially with very young children because they will not understand why they are being disciplined. With a toddler, immediate time-outs are best.

Certainly older children (five or six and older) know what they did wrong and will not forget it in an hour. What is important is that *we* don't forget. We musn't think what our children do to misbehave is lessened by time. If we do, they will get that message. They will think what they did was not that bad or that they got away with something. Be firm. Be consistent.

CHAPTER 7

The Temperament Factor

When You Think Time-Out Won't Work

Every child, every person, has a different temperament. Some parents have trouble accepting and dealing with a temperamental child.

Dana and Tom are a highly charged, dynamic couple with a high-spirited five-year-old boy named Noah. Noah often becomes difficult to handle, obstinate, and head-strong—just like his strong-willed and headstrong mom and dad. When he and his parents "get into it," sparks fly. Noah's parents thought Noah had a problem and considered taking him to a psychologist because he was so difficult to handle. When the family did go into counseling, it became evident to the therapist that the dynamics between Noah, his mother, and his father were highly charged—all the time. The therapist assessed that Noah was perfectly normal. He was simply a type A personality, just like his type A mom and dad. Noah was emulating his parents' compulsive, strong-willed behavior, and they were unable to see themselves in him. The therapist recommended some behavioral work for the parents, which eventually helped Noah.

You might be afraid to use time-out because you think it might not work. You wonder if your temperamental child will comply and remain on the time-out chair. Some parents become so intimidated by a behaviorally difficult child that they abandon a new discipline technique in fear of the child's reaction. By allowing a child to run the household, you may be creating a monstrous situation. It is imperative that you use time-out consistently. If you persist in using it, it will work after a while, even if it doesn't work perfectly the first few times. Other factors can affect a temperamentally challenging child. If you identify these factors, it will be easier to use time-out.

Age-Appropriate Behavior

Parents often discipline a child for things that are beyond the child's cognitive development. If a four-year-old toddler has an accident in his pants at nursery school or the same child can't fall asleep at nap time, these do not warrant a time-out. If you put a three-year-old on time-out for not saying please or thank you, you might be diluting the impact of time-out by disciplining your child for small things that he is not really capable of doing at that age. If that same four-year-old preschooler runs around at nap time after you've repeatedly told him to lie down quietly, then a time-out is appropriate.

Helping your child become independent and self-sufficient is great. But each age often determines what your child is ready for and what discipline is appropriate. For instance, a temper tantrum by a three-year-old is usually nothing to be worried about. Temper tantrums by a nine-year-old are another matter. You can't expect a younger child to perform like an older child or an older child to act like an adult. Children mature at different rates. When toddlers say no and pull away from us, they are not trying to be mean and insensitive. That is how toddlers act because they are trying to assert their independence and separateness from their parents. So the toddler who says no is acting age-appropriately. I would worry more if a toddler was always compliant and said "Yes, Mommy" to every request.

Three-year-old Annie loved to take things from her mother's closet and hide them. When her mother, Joyce, asked Annie where her things were, Annie would giggle and not tell her. Joyce became enraged. She was sure that Annie was a thief and would end up in a life of crime. Joyce couldn't understand that three-year-olds cannot readily distinguish a game of "taking things from Mommy's closet and hiding them" from "stealing." Moreover, what Annie was doing was age-appropriate for her young years.

Joyce needed to help Annie understand that taking things from people without asking is not okay. But she also had to realize there was nothing horrible or premeditated about her child's actions.

Some parents label age-appropriate behavior as bad or obstinate. You may think your toddler is misbehaving by having a tantrum. But most toddlers, at one time or another, will have a tantrum. You need to recognize what is excessive behavior and when a certain behavior is no longer age-appropriate.

To identify age-appropriate behavior, speak to parents that have children the same age as yours. You will be able to understand the stages your child is going through by sharing mutual experiences. In fact, you might find yourself laughing over things that you thought were "terrible" before finding out the behaviors are normal and age-appropriate.

Temper Tantrums and Other Miserable Moments

No matter how well ordered and controlled your life might be, nothing makes you feel more helpless and frustrated than a toddler lying on the floor in a public place and having a temper tantrum. Part of you would like to walk away and pretend that it is someone else's child. Another part of you probably wants to say, "Get up off that floor and knock it off!" But then there is that part of you that wants to embrace your child and make it all better.

All of your feelings are valid. Tantrums are usually appropriate for children ages five and under. Tantrums are often your child's coping mechanism. Toddlers who get over-tired, frustrated, or angry often don't have the words to express their feelings, so they do what they must to let off steam: have a tantrum. A child who gets reinforcement from a parent—even in the way of negative attention—will continue to use temper tantrums. Having tantrums becomes a very powerful tool for such children. It is their way of being independent, of saying "I'm separate from you (the parent), and I want to do things my own way."

At times, a parent and child will come together in a family tantrum, and determining who needs the time-out is difficult. Your child cries. You yell. The volume escalates. You are in the midst of a family tantrum.

If you have ever shared a temper tantrum with your child, this scene might sound familiar:

Your child screams, "No!" You raise your voice. He screams louder. You yell louder trying to tell him to calm down. He starts an all-out tirade—yelling, kicking, flailing. You lose it, pick up an object, and throw it. Your child gets more hysterical. You feel guilty, angry, frustrated, sad, and remorseful.

This temper tantrum scenario is not typical, but many parents have fallen into this behavior unwittingly.

A parent needs to learn how to try and avoid temper

tantrums and what to do when they occur. The following ideas will help you to head off a child's temper tantrum:

- Always think ahead. Some children cannot handle a lot of stimuli. Ask yourself how long you will be gone. What are the surroundings like?

- Before you take your child out for the day to run errands, ask yourself how necessary that is. Can you wait? Can you hire a baby-sitter? Can you ask a friend or neighbor to watch your child?

- Don't ask more of a young child than he can handle. Standing in a long line at a museum or movie is not a good idea. A young child who is getting whiny, bored, tired, and prepped for a tantrum will gain nothing from viewing an impressionist art show.

- If you must take your child out for the day, prepare him. Tell him where you are going and what you might be doing. Try to attach a bonus for good behavior halfway through the day and at the end of the day. For instance, stop at McDonald's for lunch, and buy your child an ice cream or a small toy at the end of the day.

- If you are going to someone's home, explain the rules of good behavior and what your expectations are. Use a lot of positive reinforcement when your child displays good behavior. Say "I really like how patient you are."

- Encourage your child to use *words*. A young child doesn't always know what to do with angry feelings and lashes out by hitting, throwing things, or having a temper tantrum.

A child who has words has an alternative. Here are some words to teach your child for when he needs to vent anger:

- "I don't like my brother when he hits me."
- "Taking my toys is not OK."
- "You make me very angry."
- "I don't want to play right now."
- "I need a time-out from you, Mommy."

Some children need a physical outlet for their anger. Recently, my daughter asked me for a punching bag. She said she needed a way to "punch out her anger" when she got really mad. At first I was reluctant, because a parent sometimes feels like any physical display is destructive. But then I realized that she *needed* to hit something, and a punching bag was a benign object. Children feel small and insignificant. A punching bag or pillow helps them let the steam out of the kettle without a blowup.

When you've tried everything and your little one falls apart in a major tantrum, you need to know what to do. Obviously, the first choice would be to put your child on time-out. But once a tantrum is happening, you are powerless to give a time-out. You need to learn how to deal with a tantrum first. Some of the following suggestions may help tame a tantrum:

- Do not yell.
- Do not try to reason with a child having a tantrum.
- Never hit your child.

- Speak in a calm voice.
- Restrain and remove your child if he is in danger of hurting himself or someone else.
- Divert your child's attention.
- Give in to your child's request if you are in a public place and the request isn't totally unreasonable.

Seven-year-old Steven kept arguing with his mother. No matter what she said, he was contrary. She felt herself getting angrier and angrier. Steven had managed to engage his mother in a verbal tug-of-war. Finally, Mom got up from the table and walked away, leaving her son dumbfounded. He was so surprised by her actions that he sat there. The argument was over.

This mom, rather than blowing up, did the best thing: she disengaged herself from an escalating situation. Trying to reason with a battling seven-year-old is futile. It will only lead to yelling and crying. By walking away, you leave a child powerless. Walking away also allows the mom to regain her composure and decide if a time-out is necessary.

Children feel secure when they know what is expected of them. A child who knows the consequences of negative behavior will be less prone to act out. If children think they can get away with something, they will. Often children know their parents' limits and know how far to push to get what they want. They manipulate and whine just enough to drive their parents sufficiently crazy so that they will acquiesce to their demands.

The Noncompliant Child

Most of the examples in this book describe the average child. But there are those children who are constantly causing a family upset by throwing tantrums, crying, whining, and refusing to comply. Parents become so frenzied over this type of behavior that they often give in to the child's demands and forego appropriate discipline. These children soon take control of the household and can cause a schism between spouses.

The father retreats. The mother feels no support. Often the fight to the time-out chair is enough to keep a parent from using time-out altogether. Giving in to a noncompliant child creates a worse situation. The more you refuse to discipline consistently, the more your child will feel powerful. A small child who is in control of his parents is not a healthy situation.

With a noncompliant, difficult child you will have to use discipline quickly, consistently, and with consequences. Difficult children need, want boundaries. Without them, they feel out of control. It is especially important to set a schedule for your child. Write it out and let your child know what he is to do and when. On the next page is a sample chart to help you set up a schedule.

This schedule will help a child with control problems stay on track. If your child refuses to follow the schedule, give him no more than twenty minutes leeway. If he doesn't comply, put him on time-out. If he still is noncompliant,

SCHEDULE
(for a six-year-old child)

	7:00	7:30	2:00–4:30	6:30	8:00
Monday–Friday	Get Dressed	Breakfast	Home Snack	Bath	Bedtime
	8:00	9:00	12:00	5:00	9:00
Saturday	Chores	Piano Lesson	Soccer	Bath	Bedtime
	9:00				8:00
Sunday	Sunday School				Bedtime

take away a privilege. Again, it is imperative that you follow through. The more your difficult child sees that you are serious, the better chance you have of staying in charge.

Parent-Child "Fit"

"Who is this kid?" Have you ever said that about your child? Does your little darling ever seem like he belongs in a different family? You and your child are like two pieces of a puzzle. Either you fit together perfectly or you just don't quite belong in each other's puzzles. The pieces don't mesh together. You probably can't figure out why. Here is your precious child—your "clone." You are raising this child in your image, and still he is nothing like you. How did this happen?

Every child, like every parent, has a unique personality. Parents often expect their children to be just like them. An artistic parent expects his child to be artistic. The intellectual and calm parent thinks his child should be this way too. That's why so many parents swell with pride when someone says, "Your little girl looks just like you."

More than looking similar, you want your child to *be* like you or better. The parent with the easy, compliant child is forever grateful when family and friends remark how well the child behaves. Somehow you think that makes you look good.

But when a child is difficult, stubborn, obstinate, and

high-strung, no one wants to lay claim to that child's behavior traits. Many couples have fought over whom their child takes after. Usually some distant relative gets the honor. In many ways, it is an honor, because spirited, difficult children more often than not turn out to be magnificent, dynamic adults. It's the road to adulthood that is bumpy. Time-out helps smooth over the bumps.

Having a child who is shy and withdrawn is disheartening when you are gregarious and social. However, these and other differences are made all the more painful when parent and child clash over their differences.

"Fit" *can* be adjusted. You are the parent, so it is up to you to compensate for parent-child differences. The most important thing we parents can do is to never make our children feel bad about who they are. Children's fragile self-esteem can diminish if they constantly hear "You're nothing like me. We can't get along. Your sister is more like me. Why can't you fit in better?" These words send the message "something is wrong with you," when in reality such children are just different from their parents.

We do better to enhance and respect our children's differences. We need to make them feel proud of who they are. Whether we like it or not, children's basic personalities are formed in vitro. We have to let them become individuals, set their boundaries but not demand they become different. Some children need social boundaries; we can let them know what is appropriate behavior and how far they can go. Use subtle methods. Encourage them.

Encourage a shy child—but don't push him to be gregarious. Children with challenging personalities especially need some "slack," or parents will constantly be reprimanding them. These children often feel that whatever they do or say will end in discipline. A negative pattern of behavior starts a downward spiral for a child who cannot always control his nature.

Recognizing your child's and your differences and respecting those differences are important. Many a quiet, complacent adult will be tempted to put a rambunctious, loud child in time-out for just being who he is. The comfort zone for one parent may be vastly different for another.

Chris, a six-year-old, is always at odds with his mother. She likes neatness. He's a mess. She wants quiet. He's loud. They never fit together well. Mom gets depressed because of the differences between Chris and her. But it is better to look for the good aspects of Chris's personality and delight in those. Learning these differences can help you to understand your child.

Learning Styles: Key to Your Child's Differences

We all have a different approach to learning and receiving information. The way we learn impacts many other ways we make decisions about how we act in the world—our interests and personality traits. It affects the way we get along with others and how we perceive things around us.

You and your child may have different learning styles. By understanding your child's learning style, you can avoid behavior problems. For instance, what we parents perceive as children "touching everything" may merely be their way of approaching the world. Their learning style is probably tactile—that is, they need to touch and feel things in order to learn about them. Other children need to learn about the world by orally explaining what they see, hear, and feel.

I have included a chart created by Howard Gardner, Ph.D., from his book *Frames of Mind* (see next page). It lists the different types of learning styles. Try to identify yours and your child's. Remember, we are a composite of different types—not just one—so don't peg your child as one type. These categories are merely a blueprint for further understanding. The more you know and understand your child, the better chance you have of disciplining him appropriately.

When All Else Fails

Tom and Judy tried everything with their six-year-old son, Randy. They used time-out, removal of privileges, positive reinforcement, and charting, but nothing seemed to really work. Randy was still unruly in school, fought with other students, and disrupted the household.

Tom and Judy bought parenting books and tried different types of discipline techniques, hoping something would work. Randy only became more defiant and obstinate.

SEVEN TYPES OF INTELLIGENCE

1. *Logical:* Pursues complex ideas. Enjoys math, puzzles, and problem solving. Is organized.

2. *Linguistic:* Learns by using words. Good with languages. Likes to read.

3. *Spatial:* Has acute visual memory. Is artistic and perceptive. Likes to invent and build things.

4. *Bodily kinetic:* Is aware of own body. Moves with skill. Responds to learning by instinct rather than logic.

5. *Musical:* Recognizes rhythm, pitch, meter, and tone. Can remember information by hearing it rather than reading it.

6. *Interpersonal:* Has great social and communication skills. Interpersonals make good speakers and leaders.

7. *Intrapersonal:* More introspective and less social. Will tend to learn and work independently.

Clearly, the situation was getting worse. Tom and Judy needed to know how to handle their son.

If your child is having trouble in school, don't wait. Talk to the teacher often. Talk to your child. Try to see if there is one specific problem or an ongoing struggle with the teacher, his friends, or both. Suggest daily progress cards be sent home for a few weeks to chart your child's behavior. Have the teacher send home an index card with the appropriate behavior checked off on one side and comments on the other side.

Progress Card

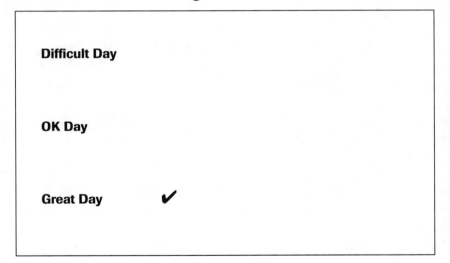

Difficult Day

OK Day

Great Day   ✔

Reward his good behavior. Do not say anything if he had a difficult day at school; ask if he would like to discuss it. It is best not to use time-out too many hours after a school incident. Also, the teacher is responsible for disciplining your child during school hours unless the problem involves physically hitting another child, stealing, or destroying property. Use the cards until you see improvement in your child's behavior.

Observe your child at home. See if he gets in fights with friends. Is he difficult to control?

When you get to the point where you have tried every reasonable discipline method and still feel helpless, the time has come to seek professional help. Professional help can come in many forms. First, prevail on your child's school. Many schools have an on-staff psychologist. Often the school can also offer testing for any learning disability that might be causing frustration and problems for your child.

If you do not want to go through the school, then seek outside counseling with a child psychologist or family therapist. Usually your pediatrician, local hospital, or mental health center can give you a list of qualified therapists, psychologists, and testing centers in your area.

There are numerous organizations that can help you with your child. Often local health clinics can offer counseling on a sliding financial scale—you pay according to what you can afford.

Do not be afraid to seek a second opinion if a doctor wants to prescribe medication for your child. This is especially true for children diagnosed with Attention Deficit Disorder (ADD). As explained in my book *The Challenging*

Child, a strong-willed child who is diagnosed with ADD may be in need of an alternative discipline method or psychotherapy, not medication. If your child is diagnosed with ADD, make sure you explore *all* possibilities. Has he been tested? Checked for a learning disability? Given a physical examination? Seen by an expert on ADD? Be your child's advocate.

There is nothing wrong with trying to use all possible means to help your child. Sometimes children do not know how to ask for help. We have to be willing to seek out what they need without fear or embarrassment from our families and friends.

CHAPTER 8

The Parent Factor

Parental Overload

You cannot implement parenting techniques if you are in a constant state of parent overload.

This became clear to Joan, who works forty hours a week and has two kids, two dogs, a husband, and an active social life. She wondered why she had been walking around screaming at everyone recently. She confessed that she hadn't taken a vacation in almost a year. Everything her kids did had begun to bother her. If her son left some toys lying around, she went ballistic. When her kids got in a fight, she acted as if they had committed a major crime. She had become short-tempered, tearful, and unable to concentrate on her work.

Everyone wants a piece of Joan's time. "I feel like people are pulling me in ten different directions," admitted Joan. "I have no time for myself at all, and I can't give enough time to my family."

Clearly, Joan is facing parent overload—sometimes referred to as *burnout*. She is trying to be supermom, super-wife, and superemployee. Although her desires to be everything to everyone are admirable, she is sacrificing herself in her pursuit of superdom. When Joan overextends herself this way, no one in her life really benefits. Her emotional state disintegrates because she feels so tired. If overload is not attended to, what can occur are conditions I term *dropout* and *drop-off.*

Drop-off is when you let one of your responsibilities drop. In most cases, especially for a woman, she "lets herself go." Women often stop taking care of themselves. Hair, makeup, nails, clothes—all of these things fall by the wayside. A woman may not even take any quiet time for herself. The family starts to expect mom to be available all the time to help with everything.

A workaholic parent will let the family drop. She doesn't take time off from work for a child's athletic game, a school play, or a day at the park. The point is, whatever you give up, someone usually suffers—you, your child, your spouse.

Many couples' marriages suffer when they find that they have no private time together. One woman admitted, "I can't remember the last time my husband and I made love. Between work, meetings, kids, and the house, it's like two ships passing in the night. We both collapse in bed at the end of the day with nothing more on our minds than sleeping." If you are at this point, a red light should go off in your head. There's danger ahead.

The problem is, most of us get into such a conditioned pattern of behavior that we fail to see how much trouble we are in until it is too late. Once we reach overload, a major blowup can occur that can impact our marriage, our job, and our relationship with our kids.

Once you have reached full overload you can go into dropout: feeling you "can't take it anymore," you drop out of your life. By this, I mean you choose to make a 180-degree turnaround. Instead of being superparent, you do not participate in your child's activities. You can become uninterested in the lives of those around you. You may jeopardize your job and quit or get fired. Your marriage may fall apart, or ultimately you may fall apart.

Although dropout is the *extreme,* it can happen if you don't attend to your inner needs. By the time you hit dropout, you need a parental time-out. You need to attend to yourself by reevaluating your priorities. Here are some things to focus on:

+ Take a vacation.

+ Set your priorities.

+ Communicate your feelings and needs to your family.

+ Break old patterns. Don't play martyr; ask for help.

+ Work on time management.

There are things you can do to avoid overload so you can be a more effective person and parent.

Overtalk

Did you ever start lecturing your child, only to see her eyes slowly glaze over and her expression start to look like she is a million miles away? You have become a victim of what Dr. Thomas Phelan refers to in his manual, *1-2-3 Magic!*, as the no-talking rule. You are making the mistake of trying to *convince* your child that she must follow your rules, as opposed to the better idea that she must follow the rules because you are the parent and you know what is better for your child than she does.

Arguments with a child can go around in circles and end up nowhere. Lecturing toddlers is totally useless because they will not understand most of what you say and will forget the next minute.

Although always acknowledging your child's feelings is important, you don't want to minimize a misbehavior by talking and then "hoping" your child learned a lesson from your lecture. If you want to make an impact on your child, make your words short and to the point.

The following examples may give you an idea of short talk to use when your child misbehaves:

- "Your behavior is inappropriate."
- "No!" (*Say it only once.*)
- "I respect your feelings, but my rules stand."
- "Because I said so."
- "I've made my decision."
- "You have until the count of ten."

When our children learn our short talk, they'll know we mean business when we use it.

Walk Away

Remember, by walking away from a child, a parent makes a huge impact. Our children want our attention all the time. They need and want our reassurance and praise. What your child doesn't have over you is power. You are the big cheese. You are bigger, stronger, and smarter, so never forget it.

I once saw a three-year-old running her ragged mother around in circles. The toddler was barking orders at her mom, who complied with the child's demands. In essence, the mother had given her power away. She was literally in a sweat trying to make her toddler happy. This task was virtually impossible. Finally, the mother became angry and screamed at her child. The child, clearly the winner in this battle, knew instinctively how to manipulate Mom to get what she wanted. The mom was "hooked in." She needed to disconnect, and at that point the only way would have been to walk away to keep her power as a parent. If your child starts to escalate or manipulate or whine and, after one warning, doesn't stop, *walk away.*

Pushing Your Child's Limits

When Susan and her little girl, Jana, were shopping at a very exclusive boutique in Manhattan, the four-year-old decided to have a major tantrum because she wasn't allowed to touch the $5,000 Chanel dress on the mannequin. That prohibition might seem reasonable to most people. But to Jana, who had fallen in love with the chiffon and imported lace, it was totally unfair. After all, that dress was *sooo* pretty. Susan gave Jana a time-out and then, after much aggravation, left the store.

Now, I do not advocate allowing a child to touch an expensive dress. However, I also do not advocate taking a child on a shopping trip to an exclusive boutique, where the temptation to touch the lovely items may be too overwhelming. A child who feels you are being unfair is probably right. Although children should not be allowed to destroy other people's things, roam free in a store, touch what they like, or throw tantrums when they don't get their way, it is unfair to put young children in an inappropriate environment and then punish them for acting their age.

You wouldn't take your toddler to an important business meeting. Then why take her to a chic boutique or fancy restaurant and expect her to act differently? When you do, you are pushing your child's limits.

To make requests of our children when they are out with us is certainly OK. They should use manners, be polite, and follow our rules. But remember what I discussed about age-appropriate behavior: children are not little adults. They act according to their age and instincts. Do not expect more.

Another problem with pushing children is what is referred to as the "bewitching hour" syndrome. Perhaps this scenario sounds familiar. It is five-thirty in the evening.

Mom is in the shopping mall or grocery store or someplace similar. Her child is tired, hungry, and cranky.

The child says, "I want to go!" The mother says, "I have just one more errand to run."

The child whines, "I want to go home!" The mom responds, "OK, honey. Let me just finish one more thing."

Suddenly, without warning, the child freaks out. The mother loses her cool (since she is tired, hungry, and cranky, too). She puts the child on time-out, which by this time is probably useless. The two of them go home in a frenzy; the child is miserable and so is the mom.

All of us have been there. We push our children past their limits and are upset when they misbehave. Children can't always express their feelings, so it is up to us parents to read their signals. A hungry, tired three-year-old does not have the ability to wait until you run one more errand. Her nervous system is finished. That's it. She will break down, and it doesn't matter where you are or what you are doing.

Of course, accommodating your child may not be possible at all times, but coming prepared is best. Take along extra food, a favorite toy, perhaps a cassette of some soothing music to play in the car. Take ten minutes and let your child rest, eat, and relax. Children feel their parent's harried pace and tension. They pick up on all our signals and act accordingly.

If you can avoid it, do not push past the "bewitching hour." Do what you have to do another day. Usually that one last thing can wait. Delaying your gratification in order to avoid your child's misery is certainly worth inconvenience.

Time-Out Teamwork

Parents need to be a brick wall, a monolith, an impenetrable barrier that no little tyke can chip away and tear down. If this seems dramatic, think again.

Here's a typical family scenario. Your little five-year-old gets angry, throws her toy against the wall, and chips the paint. You get furious and send her to time-out. The child gets hysterical and runs to your spouse, begging to be forgiven and not put in time-out. She cries and whines. Your spouse gets upset and tries to comfort the child. You scream at your spouse, "I told her to go to time-out. Don't talk to her." The child acts frightened. Your spouse tells you to calm down. You get angrier and tell your spouse to "stay out of it!" Your spouse gets angry, and the two of you go at it.

While your little one has won the war, you and your spouse are still fighting your battle. The child doesn't get disciplined because of the conflict created between the two adults, and the parent teamwork has broken down. Your child sees you as a divided force and now knows how to get what she wants. What this type of scenario creates is:

- A division between the spouses

- An unclear picture of what is expected of the child

- Poor role modeling for the child

- Anger and resentment between the spouses

If you plan to institute time-out in your home, that you and your spouse become a team is vital. Work together on discipline techniques. Most important, if you decide to use time-out, discuss, read, and find out how to use it properly together. If one parent uses time-out and the other doesn't, it is useless. You will totally confuse your child.

Also, never contradict one another in front of your child. If you disagree with your spouse's choice of discipline, discuss it in private. You need to support one another and let your child know that Mommy and Daddy are a team. Otherwise, your child will drive a wedge between the two of you and break down the weakest parent. Again, disagreeing with one another is OK, but not in front of your child. Do it in private. Constant disagreement about discipline is not healthy for a marriage, a child, or a family.

The important factor is to mirror your spouse by using statements that give the clear message that you are a team. Make sure you use the word *we* when your child starts to disagree with one of you.

The Team Support Statements (page 94) will help you deal with your child when the team starts to break up.

Private Time

Some couples spend so much time working and parenting that they forget about each other. The stress of disciplining your child can wear on a relationship. Often a child interferes with your private time, especially if you always make that child your first priority. A family is made up of adults

TEAM SUPPORT STATEMENTS

- Dad/Mom and I are a team.

- We respect each other's decisions.

- Your father/mother and I will discuss this matter later and decide if we should handle this differently.

- We see your point of view.

- We support each other.

- We understand how you feel.

and children. Everyone, *including the adults,* needs to be nurtured, loved, spoiled, and attended to.

That you take private time with your spouse is important for the overall health of your family. Private time means getting a baby-sitter and going out together alone. It means going away, even overnight, to a hotel and rekindling the romance in your relationship.

A parent, especially one with a small child, sometimes feels forgotten. A woman may still be struggling to get her postbaby weight down and is often too harried to spend a few hours to herself. Conversely, a man may feel like a third wheel in the household; men are often shoved aside for baby and child tasks. It is not easy when you and your spouse both are juggling home, careers, appointments, practices, and screaming and cranky kids.

Who wants to get sexy at 10 P.M. when the kids are still whining for you to chase away the bogeyman and your toddler refuses to go into her own bed?

Think of private time as a necessity. Don't make excuses and procrastinate. Months, maybe years, might pass before you and your spouse go away together. By that time, you may have lost some of the intimacy of your relationship.

If you do finally make some time together, follow these guidelines:

- Talk about the kids only once a day, for no more than one-half hour.

- Don't complain.

- Hold hands and kiss.

- Try to please each other—be romantic.

- Do not go to a family resort. Find a romantic hideaway.

- Call home only once, if you feel the urge; otherwise, if you are only going away for one or two nights, don't call.

- Do not make sex the priority of the trip. Let it evolve naturally without a "let's hurry and do it while we can" attitude.

- Have fun together. You might have forgotten how.

Private time is essential to the health of your marriage. Don't ever feel selfish or neglectful of your child if you need time to yourself. A happy and relaxed person makes a better parent.

Parental Time-Outs

Taking time-outs for yourself is important. This applies to all areas of your life. You need to stop and take a time-out whenever you start to feel exhausted, scattered, short-tempered, overly sensitive, and inattentive. Ask your family and friends to help you by being your barometer. Sometimes we fail to see what's happening to ourselves until it's too late.

When you take a time-out, you have to let your family know that you are off-limits. The household will not fall apart without you for a few hours—even for a day. People are surprisingly resilient, especially children when we empower them to be independent. You can say "I need a time-out. Please do not disturb me until _____. Then I can help you with whatever you need." Be definitive—and don't back down.

Taking a time-out can mean a few hours alone, soaking in a bath and listening to music, getting a massage, or doing any activity that relaxes you. You should also take extended time-outs in the form of vacations. Some parents never vacation away from their children. Of course, this is an individual choice, but personally I recommend short vacations (weekends) when your child is an infant and toddler and longer vacations (a week) when your child is school age (over six). Surprisingly enough, children do quite well while parents are away. The key to parent vacations is finding someone who will use time-out with your child while you are away.

A friend of mine once told me, "From the moment you

have a child, you never truly relax for the rest of your life." At first, I thought this seemed like a negative affirmation, but then I realized that what she said had some truth to it. You worry when your new baby cries for no reason. You wonder why she isn't interested in potty training. You are stressed if your toddler throws tantrums. You are concerned about your child's schoolwork, first camp experience, and first date. Will she be happy? Will she do well? Will you be a good parent? Will you overlook some important detail in her development?

Let's face it. Parenthood is a total joy. But it is a big, important job that requires a lot from you. That is why I stress taking time-outs for yourself.

This is especially true when you have a new baby in the house. The demands and stress of having an infant can leave you totally drained. Once your baby becomes a toddler, you will need even more energy. Keeping up with an active three-year-old *is work*. This is the time when your patience may wear thin and you can lose your temper easily. If you do not see the danger signs of impending burnout, then you will not be able to parent as effectively.

As soon as you feel as if you are "losing it," take a time-out. Excuse yourself and say "Mom/Dad needs a time-out to think things over. When I am calm, I will deal with you." Sometimes just removing yourself from an escalating situation can calm a child down. Often, a child will play off of a parent. She'll whine, tantrum, and complain only when you are around. So a parental time-out sends the message "I am disconnecting." Your child then has to use some of her inner resources to get in control.

I am also highly in favor of time-outs for parents with quick tempers. A potentially volatile situation can be averted by taking time-out before doing something you'll be sorry for. If you are feeling out of control, tell your spouse or a friend or neighbor to watch your child. The point is, if you lose it, so will your child.

Here are guidelines for parental time-out:

- When you feel overstressed or out of control, take a time-out.
- Tell your child, "I need to take a time-out for myself. I will be back in a few minutes." Go someplace quiet, shut the door behind you, take a deep breath, and close your eyes.
- Try to limit the time-out to ten minutes. Otherwise, your child might feel anxious or worried about your departure.
- When you return, say "I finished my time-out, and I feel better now."
- Continue to deal with the problem but in a quiet, rational manner. If your child's behavior warrants it, say "Now it is your turn for a time-out."

Letting Go of Expectations

A child is not an adult. This might sound like an obvious statement, but it is not. Parents often treat their children as miniadults, expecting behavior that the child is incapable of. For example, we tend to expect our children to be sensitive and reasonable. Many mothers have come to me with complaints of their child's insensitivity and lack of compassion. I, myself, couldn't understand it when my four-year-old daughter didn't understand that I needed time to myself. Couldn't *she see* I was exhausted? Why was she so whiny and insensitive? What I wanted was for her to say "OK, Mommy, you rest and relax while I go play quietly." Getting an adult to respond that way is difficult enough, let alone a child.

Young children are basically narcissistic, give-me, get-me little beings whose world revolves around themselves. This is normal behavior until the children start becoming aware of the world around them. In fact, children are often cognizant of and sensitive to outside factors before becoming sensitive to parents and siblings. How many times have you seen your little one cry at a hurt puppy or a dead goldfish? Partly this is because children feel so comfortable and safe in a home environment that they know they can "break down" and be themselves without judgment or fear of reprisals. This is actually healthy behavior on the part of a child. It's you, the parent, who needs to let go.

We parents expect a lot from our children because we see them as extensions of ourselves. In many ways they are. But they have their own thoughts, feelings, ideas, and personalities. If a child does something wrong, that doesn't mean the parent did something wrong.

As children become more aware of themselves, they

learn that the parent is a separate being. A parent needs to have this same awareness. Letting go is the first step toward raising an independent child. Empowering our children with a sense of self-sufficiency is a step in helping them to make their way in an often difficult and complex world. Be close by to help, to guide, and to nurture, but don't smother or make demands on your child. You will only create a clingy, insecure child or an angry, rebellious one. The most important gift parents can give their children is the freedom to be themselves.

Sometimes the best way to avoid conflict is to "let it go." By this, I mean pick your battles. It is not worth the aggravation and upset in your household to discipline children for every little thing they do wrong. Children *need* to do things wrong. That's how they learn.

John constantly reprimanded his son about how the boy poured the catsup and used a fork. John said he made a mess and poured too fast. As a result, the boy felt anxious every time he sat down at the kitchen table. He refused to do anything for himself. If you want to teach your child the correct way to pour and hold utensils, that's fine. But to put a child on time-out for not pouring catsup properly is not appropriate.

This applies to things such as a toddlers' messing their clothes. Let it go. I remember someone telling me that "little kids have little problems" and "big kids have bigger problems." No words were ever truer. So save your energy for the big problems, because you'll need it.

Raising a very challenging little girl, I could have had her on time-out every ten minutes. But I realized that something was not working or she wouldn't need to go on time-out so often. I made a list of behavior priorities. The priorities were listed in order of importance. If these priorities were abused, then I put my daughter on time-out. I also made a list of things I was willing to let go of.

Every list will be different according to the child's age, although there are basic behaviors for all children. The list should be based on your personal values and rules. But for every rule you enforce, you have to be willing to let something go.

Some temperamentally difficult children may need you to let more things go. This may seem odd, but difficult children need more rope or else they will never get a break from disciplinary action. This inevitably impacts their self-esteem.

The sample Priorities List will give you a basic idea of some of the things you might want to enforce and let go. Making such a list will help you decide what your priorities are and where to ease up. Also, you can assess each situation and ask yourself: "How many times has this happened before?" "Is this a dangerous situation?" "How important is it to make my point?" "Is this an opportunity to teach my child an important lesson?"

Fill in the chart, check the appropriate boxes, and indicate frequency (once a week, more than twice a week, etc.). Fill in the behaviors that bother you, and refer to the chart if you need to impose time-out or let go more.

PRIORITIES LIST

Behavior	Frequency	Let Go	Time-Out
Spilled milk	four times this week		✓
Forgot to take a bath	once this week	✓	
Hit his brother	frequently		✓
Won't share toys	frequently		✓
Kicks dog	frequently		✓
Didn't put toys away	twice this week	✓	
Forgot to brush teeth	twice this week	✓	

What Is Important?

You need to decide which behaviors are most important, or your child might never get out of the time-out chair. You will have to choose the behaviors according to your child's temperament. If your little one is constantly whining and talking back, then that might take precedence over not picking up toys. For some parents, completing chores might be more important than not going to bed on time. Every child and every parent are different, and what works for one family might not work for another.

At some point you will have to be willing to let some things go. Children need to explore their worlds, make mistakes, and learn from their own actions. By doing so, they create an internal sense of right and wrong and make behavioral choices by how they will be judged by their parents, their peers, and society in general. This is the first step to developing a conscience.

Sending children to time-out for every minor transgression can be hurtful to their self-esteem. They will view themselves as bad children, and this is not the message we want to give them.

Key Behaviors

Certain behaviors, I believe, should not be overlooked. These are key behaviors that affect the child's interactions with other members of society and form his core personality.

Priority Checklist

List what behaviors you want to work on in order of importance, and write down the desired change.

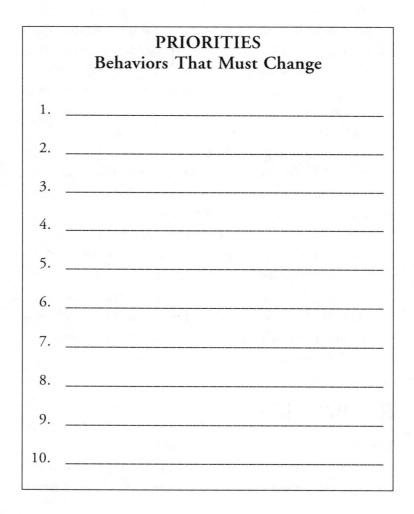

PRIORITIES
Behaviors That Must Change

1. _____

2. _____

3. _____

4. _____

5. _____

6. _____

7. _____

8. _____

9. _____

10. _____

A child can get a reputation for having a bad attitude and being a troublemaker if the parent doesn't get these behaviors in check. If your child displays any of these behaviors, you must *never* let it go by. Immediately put your child on time-out and discuss the inappropriateness of the behavior. You may need to get further help if the following behaviors occur repeatedly:

- Lying
- Cheating
- Stealing
- Hitting, fighting, and pushing
- Teasing and hurting another child's feelings
- Talking back and rude behavior

Using the Priority Checklist, rank in order of importance the behaviors you want your child to change.

Role Models

Children are sponges that love to soak up everything around them. A parent is a child's primary bond and role model. Whatever you do, your child will emulate it in some form, either verbally or by action.

When you call time-out, you are removing the child from any form of verbal or physical abuse. Your child is given a chance to think about what she did, calm down, and then start fresh.

The best gift—and it is called a gift because it is so special—is to be a good role model for your child. I know this is often a lot to ask. You are not an automaton that says and does everything perfectly. But that is not what good modeling is about.

A lot of role modeling is about feelings. Being able to talk to your child and to open up good lines of communication is your primary objective.

I remember a time when my daughter, Alexandra, who was about seven at the time, and I were grocery shopping. A woman, who had a daughter about the same age as Alexandra, took an apple from the produce section and ate it. She then proceeded to eat some grapes. My daughter asked me if she could have an apple, too. I said, "Let's weigh it and pay for it first." I explained that eating food from a grocery store is not OK unless you pay for it.

That same woman and her daughter later stood in line in front of us at the checkout counter. The little girl grabbed a candy bar and proceeded through the checkout line and out the door. When the cashier mentioned that the girl had taken the candy, the mother was aghast. She spanked the little girl and told her, "Never take anything from a store." The little girl walked out hysterical.

My daughter looked up at me. "But the mommy took some fruit and didn't pay." Here was an opportunity to model good behavior by using this real-life example.

Obviously, you will find numerous ways to model good behavior, based on your own values and family life. But the Parents' Checklist (see next page) represents the basis for modeling that applies to all children. It is based on respect, trust, and fairness.

Modeling skills, along with the use of time-out, form parenting skills that can greatly reduce anger, frustration, and behavioral problems in your child.

PARENTS' CHECKLIST FOR GOOD ROLE MODELING

☐ Say "I'm sorry."

☐ Do not use swearwords in front of your child.

☐ If you are in a bad mood, say so.

☐ Take time-outs for yourself.

☐ Never cheat or steal.

☐ Show kindness to others.

☐ Admit your mistakes.

☐ Don't have temper tantrums.

☐ Never hit another person.

☐ Practice good manners.

☐ Listen.

☐ Be a good friend.

☐ Talk. Don't yell.

☐ If you tell a "white lie," explain why.

☐ Be fair and not judgmental.

☐ Read.

☐ Don't be a couch potato.

CHAPTER 9

Bed, Bath, Bananas, and Beyond

When it comes to battles about meals, bath, and bedtime, my best advice is to not get involved in power struggles.

One concerned mother expressed her dismay to her son's pediatrician. "He won't eat bananas, and I can't get him to take a bath every night. I'm beside myself. What's going to happen to my son?" The doctor quietly replied, "I wouldn't worry. No child has ever come to me for banana deficiency and a dirty body." He also reminded her that her son was a strapping, quite healthy four-year-old and that she must be doing something right.

Kids aren't neurotic. Parents are. We worry and fret about children's eating, sleeping, potty training, and bathing as if these are the most important issues of their young lives. Children who understand that we parents are not emotionally attached to these issues will not fight us on them. Sleeping and eating are instinctive behaviors; they don't have to be taught. Certainly a child should not be disciplined for not meeting the parents' desires in these areas. The minute your child detects that there is *enormous* importance in eating carrots, he will turn orange before eating veggies. These are areas where you will need to "let it go," or you will create more of a problem than you already have. The only time you should be concerned is if your child is losing weight or is continually ill or is tired and yawning all day.

Bed — Sleep-Time Rituals

Bedtime can be a very unpleasant experience for some parents. Joyce confessed that a half an hour before her son's bedtime, she became extremely anxiety-ridden. "I knew he was going to whine and cry and refuse to go to bed," she complained. "It was a nightly struggle with my three-year-old. He never got to bed on time or without a tantrum."

Joyce had bedtime jitters. She needed to find the proper time and environment for her son's bedtime ritual. *Ritual* is what bedtime should be for a child. A child needs sameness— the same blanket, the same bed, the same time, the same teddy bear, the same song, the same story. This might sound boring to you, but it will make your little one feel secure.

Bedtime can be a scary time for children. They are put in a dark room with shadows and lights flickering on the walls. Their little imaginations think they see monsters. Under the bed is a hand just waiting to grab them. Every small sound is magnified. Mommy and Daddy are asleep, and they feel lonely and frightened. It is up to *you* to set up a cozy, inviting, secure environment for your child.

Here is a list of some tried-and-true ways to help your child cope with sleep difficulties. You can use all or just one of these methods:

- Use a night-light.

- Play soft, mellow music—no rock or rap.

- Have your child take a warm bath before bedtime.

- Read a benign story, nothing having to do with violence, monsters, or scary situations.

- Rub your child's back.

- Make sure your child has a transitional object: a blanket, stuffed animal, or something familiar and comforting. This also is good for school-age children. Children as old as ten or eleven often sleep with a stuffed animal or baby blanket.

- Stay with your child, hold his hand, sing a lullaby or favorite song.

- Create a bedtime routine. Try to establish the same rituals every night until your child is comfortable.

- Unless you are an advocate of the family bed, inviting your child into your bed is not a good idea unless he has experienced a trauma (illness, a bad nightmare, earthquake).

- Make your caretaker or baby-sitter aware of your child's nighttime ritual and ask that it be implemented.

- Be sensitive to your child's signals. Illness, transitions, new surroundings, problems in school—all these things can cause sleep problems. Give some extra care and TLC during times of change and stress.

- Be consistent. Try to establish a set bedtime for your child every night. Do not deviate or allow an extra ten minutes for this or that. Attempts to get you to deviate are manipulative. If you give in, your child will find a reason to stay up past bedtime every night. Be firm.

- Use positive-strokes incentives for poky kids. Tell your child that if he gets ready for bed quickly, you can read two stories. Set the timer and give two-minute warnings.

- Praise good behavior.

Do not give time-outs in the middle of the night. This is disruptive. If your child continually gets out of bed, take points off his chart. Warn that continuing to get out of bed will cause you to take privileges away.

Some children have trouble falling asleep. You can't make someone fall asleep, so as long as your child is in bed, leave him alone. *Do not* go into a child's room and tell him to "go to sleep." Let him fall asleep naturally. Some children need less sleep than others. Eventually children will fall into a sleep rhythm, and their bodies will tell them what they need.

Bath—It's OK to Be Dirty Sometimes

Getting a child to bathe has to be based on "dirt assessment." This means that you must determine just how dirty and smelly your little one is and how big a fight you are willing to engage in.

Some activities such as mud play or sports play should make a bath nonnegotiable, and your child should get a time-out for noncompliance. If your child has not been playing in the mud or playing sports and is *sooo* tired that he just can't drag his little body into the tub, be willing to say OK. You need to determine for your child what is acceptable and unacceptable bath behavior.

As you do for bedtime, you should establish certain bath-time rituals. For instance:

* Bathe five (three, six) times a week.

* The parent chooses the bath days.

* Bath time lasts at least five minutes and no longer than twenty minutes.

* Hair gets washed (x) times a week.

* Sponge bathe on nonbath days.

This is only a sample schedule. You need to set up your own rules according to what is comfortable for your child. But discuss your child's bath schedule ahead of time so he will not be surprised. Try to make bath time as much fun as possible. Toys, rubber duckies, funny soaps, and sponges can help.

It is also important that your child understand that he must wash his face and hands in the morning, after play, and before meals. These requirements should be nonnegotiable and should become habit for your child. This establishes good hygiene habits.

If your child *flatly* refuses to take a bath or follow your rules, use time-out.

Bananas — Your Child Will Eat

Have you ever seen adults trying to get a child to eat food? Most of the dialogue revolving around food comes in the form of pleading and cajoling:

- "Please try the cauliflower. You'll love it."
- "Just a tiny little bite. I'll give you dessert after you take a bite."
- "Cauliflower will make you strong so you can be a good athlete."
- "Eat your cauliflower or you will get a time-out."

If any of the above sounds familiar, then you have joined the ranks of normal parents. You want to be a good parent, and you serve healthy, nutritionally well-balanced meals that are not full of sugars and fats. But you feel as though you are failing in your duty because your child refuses most of what you serve.

The first step to getting a child to eat is to stop arguments or discussions about food. Parents' obsessing about food only makes a child want to resist more. Setting rules around mealtimes is important, but you do not want to be a drill sergeant. Be clear and specific. Set the food down in front of your child. Try to present it in a way that might interest a child. For instance, I bought a delicious low-fat buttermilk salad dressing. I put it on my vegetables and suggested my daughter try the same thing. She hesitated at first but then dipped a piece of broccoli in the dressing. Needless to say, she is now a veggie eater. If your child likes catsup on everything, fine. Some kids want peanut butter on all of their food. This can't hurt them. It may not appeal to you, but you're not a child.

Ann, a mother of two, recalled, "When my children were toddlers and even up until they were five or six years, I would sometimes serve their meals in a muffin tin. I put something different in each of the six cups. It's just a fun way of presenting the meal, but the kids loved it." Each meal becomes an adventure this way.

Try to be as creative as possible, and don't attach stigmas to what your child likes to eat. Remember, there still is a piece of broccoli under the glob of salad dressing even though it may be disguised.

Many doctors agree that if you offer well-balanced meals, a child somehow gets the proper nutrition. Your child is entitled to have likes and dislikes, just as you do. Try to be firm yet tolerant of your child's preferences. Talking about good nutrition with your child is OK, but you don't want to

MEALTIME RULES

+ No eating snacks right *before* dinner.

+ No eating after dinner except dessert.

+ Take *one* bite of any new food.

+ Time-out for sneaking a dessert without having eaten a portion of the meal.

+ Time-out for throwing or playing with food.

+ No "special" foods prepared: everyone gets the same meal.

+ Use good manners at the table.

do it in a way that will make him feel guilty. Don't say "Thousands of homeless children would love your peas." This is a below-the-belt tactic. Also, your child might offer up these peas. Follow your good instincts and remember:

+ Don't force a child to eat.

+ Give a few choices once or twice a week.

+ Use time-out for major food infractions such as throwing or spitting food.

+ Involve your child in food preparation.

You should hold firm about certain rules. Go over the rules with your child, and let him know a time-out will be given if he breaks these rules. Also, children who throw a tantrum at the meal table should be picked up physically and removed to the time-out chair. They should not be allowed to return to the table. Let them know meal time is over. They won't starve! Rules can be adjusted for your child, home, and lifestyle. No rules are written in stone.

Dressing Up and Down

Six-year-old Suzie loves to do everything but get dressed. She likes to brush her hair for twenty minutes and play in the sink and play and play and play until her harried mother comes rushing in half-crazed. Mom yells at Suzie, "Why aren't you dressed? Hurry up. You'll be late for school." Suzie pokes along. She plays with her shoelaces and can't decide what ribbon to put around her hair. Ten minutes later, her mother calls, "Suzie, we have to go now! Did you finish breakfast?" But Suzie hasn't even finished getting dressed. By this time Mom is yelling, screaming, and threatening. Suzie is late for school, and her mom is late for work. Clearly a better way must be found to solve the dressing problem.

Probably the most important thing to do is to make sure your child knows *how* to dress himself. Some children haven't a clue how to button buttons, tie laces, and zip zippers. But by the end of kindergarten, your child should have everything down pat.

Always set out your child's clothes the night before school or if you have to be ready at a specified time in the morning.

Write out or use pictures (for a younger child) of the

morning ritual. Go over this routine with your child often. Be brief. For example:

1. Get up.
2. Brush your teeth.
3. Wash your face.
4. Put on clothes lying on the chair.
5. Eat breakfast.

Children totally lose track of time. Parents can use time-out timers to help move them along. Set the timer for about twenty minutes. This should be enough time for a child to get dressed. At first your child will think that only a minute went by, but eventually his "inner" timer will know what twenty minutes are and he will finish in time.

If your child does not comply after a number of timed attempts, take off points from his chart or take away a privilege. If your child throws a tantrum or becomes obstinate, put him on time-out as well.

In the beginning, be sure to check on your child after five or ten minutes to help keep him on task. Also, give lots of positive strokes if your child finishes dressing by the time the timer dings.

One last suggestion. I don't suggest you let your child watch television while dressing, eating, or going to bed. A child gets mesmerized by television, loses track of time, and gets nothing accomplished. Television should be a privilege at an appropriate time. When your child gets dressed on time, be sure to give lots of praise.

CHAPTER 10

Questions
and Answers

I have spoken with hundreds of parents about time-out and other parenting issues. In this chapter I try to provide answers to some key questions that parents want addressed. Remember, every situation and every child are different. These answers are not definitive but rather are a guideline for parents to follow when dealing with similar issues.

Q. When is the best time to start time-out?

A. Two-and-a-half years old. Before that age, a child usually does not have the cognitive development to understand what you are doing. By two-and-a-half years of age, children have a better command of language and a better developed sense of being separate from the parent. Although there is nothing wrong with telling younger toddlers that their behavior is "not OK," using time-out may not sink in.

Q. Can I change where we use time-out?

A. Not in your home. Try to be consistent and use time-out in the same place. Also try to use the same chair. Do not pick a place where your child might become distracted.

Q. My eight-year-old refuses to go to the time-out chair. He is too big to physically carry over. What should I do?

A. Go immediately to removal of privileges. He'll get the point, and most likely he'll be willing to go to time-out the next time he misbehaves.

Q. My three-year-old loves to go to time-out. What am I doing wrong?

A. Nothing. Time-out for a younger child can be a way to separate her from an escalating situation or from negative behavior. A child may need time-out for a "cooldown," and young children especially may not have the cognitive ability to pull themselves away from a negative situation. By giving time-outs, parents are helping them to do so. Make sure, however, that you are not giving a time-out in a bedroom or playroom. A time-out should be in a benign hallway or entryway.

Q. When my daughter was four, she used to listen and get scared when I put her on time-out. Now she's almost seven, and she doesn't listen or respond as well. Help!

A. As children grow, they change. So the limits you impose on them will need to change also. What worked for a toddler may not work so well for a seven-year-old. Reassess your limits. Go over the rules for your child so she is very clear about what is expected of her. Let her know the consequences for misbehavior. Follow through quickly and consistently.

Q. My three-year-old daughter was the flower girl at my sister's wedding. She refused to go down the aisle alone and then started crying when we prodded her. It was terrible. I put my daughter on time-out afterwards, but she was hysterical. Now my cousin wants her to be a flower girl.

A. Three-year-olds are too young to be put in pressure situations where they are asked to perform. Sometimes time-out is not the answer. You can't blame a child for age-appropriate three-year-old behavior. Your daughter might have been scared or tired by the time the ceremony began. I would politely decline the flower girl offer until your child is older and understands what is happening. If an adult or older child wants to walk down with her, that might alleviate the problem, but I wouldn't push her into the situation.

Q. My six-year-old keeps giving his baby brother inappropriate toys with small pieces to play with. I keep telling him not to, but he says he wants to share with his brother. Any suggestions?

A. Yes. A six-year-old is mature enough to know what it means when Mommy says "Don't give that to your brother. It is dangerous." Put your son on time-out if he does it again, and let him know that wanting to share is very nice, but you'll help him pick out appropriate toys to share with his brother.

Q. It seems as if I argue with my four-year-old over everything. I say one thing, and she does the opposite. I'm exhausted. What should I do to make my life easier?

A. First, are you arguing over insignificant things? With a child, it is best to only deal with important issues. Focus on changing one behavior before you take on ten. With one behavior you can be more consistent, and chances are that as one behavior improves, so will others. If she continues to argue, use time-out. You are the boss.

Q. My four-year-old kicks the wall when he is on time-out. What should I do?

A. Let him know that kicking the wall will not be tolerated. Tell him that if he kicks the wall, you will reset the timer for another four minutes. This should work. Otherwise, put the time-out chair in the middle of the room. He can kick the air.

Q. I feel like a single parent. I'll discipline my child and follow through with time-out, but my spouse rarely does. What to do?

A. Both parents need to administer discipline in order for it to be effective. Otherwise, the child gets the message that one of you is not really serious, and she may feel it is okay to misbehave because there won't always be consequences. Tell your spouse that you need support and discuss the time-out prescription, how and when to use it, and other methods in the book. Arm your spouse with the necessary parenting information. Remind your spouse that it is in your child's best interest to parent as partners.

Q. I put my child on time-out in a corner of the grocery store. I stood a few feet away. Two ladies gave me such a dirty look, as if I were a horrible mother. I stopped the time-out because I got so uncomfortable. Was I wrong?

A. Yes. What would those ladies have done if they had seen you scream at or smack your child? What you did, give a time-out, was appropriate and a much better alternative to other more harsh methods. Don't let other people make you feel bad about your parenting. Stay strong. Use time-out in public places if you have to!

Q. My five-year-old will eat only peanut butter. He flatly refuses anything else. I'm in a panic. Will he get sick?

A. I suggest you put out the evening meal and stop accommodating your child's eating whims. Try a lot of different foods presented in interesting ways. Even if he only picks a little, that's OK. Don't force him to eat, but let him know that you will be serving a variety of foods at dinner. If he screams or whines, put him on time-out. Do not engage in power struggles. Let him decide to eat on his own. Be willing to give him peanut butter for lunch. Don't make him go completely cold turkey. Even once a week for dinner is OK.

Q. When I warn my child three or four times that she will get a time-out if she keeps misbehaving, she says she's sorry and begs me not to put her on time-out. Usually I feel bad and don't put her on time-out. But she often continues to misbehave. Is it too late to put her on time-out?

A. Absolutely not. But you should have put her on time-out after one warning. She also needs boundaries set. She knows that she can push you far enough and you will give in and not put her on time-out. Don't wait. Let her know that bad behavior will not be allowed. Let her know you love her but she will still go to time-out.

Q. My mother-in-law does not want to use time-out. She has spanked my five-year-old and six-year-old sons. This really upsets me. How should I handle this?

A. You must communicate to your mother-in-law that time-out is the discipline method you use in your home and that you will not allow her to spank your children. Discuss time-out with her, why you use it, and how you use it. Try to persuade her to use time-out with your children.

Q. My four-year-old child will undress while sitting on the time-out chair. This upsets me, and a number of times I have interrupted the time-out and gotten her dressed again. What can I do to stop this behavior?

A. You have a clever little girl. But you are smarter. Do nothing. She wants to upset you. Continue to ignore her, and if she gets up off of the chair, reset the timer. She might get a little chilly sitting on the chair without clothes and decide it's not such a good idea.

Q. What makes time-out effective?

A. Time-out is thoroughly boring. When a little child sits for four, five, or six minutes, it is like an eternity. There is nothing to do but to calm down, because all stimuli and anger have been removed.

Q. My six-year-old daughter always tells little "stories," but I call them lies. She exaggerates things, and quite frankly I sometimes get embarrassed. What should I do?

A. Explain to your daughter the differences between truth and untruth. Do not overreact when you hear a story, but explain that it is not OK to lie. Tell her that friends might not trust her if they think she tells stories that aren't true. Also, if your daughter likes telling stories, suggest she say "This is a story, but it is not true." It is nice to have a good imagination but socially necessary to be able to distinguish truth from lies.

Q. My third grader has very low self-esteem. He never thinks anything he does is good enough. What should I do to help him?

A. First, find out if your child is having trouble with his work at school. If he is, then you need to address that problem first. If he is just *feeling* as though nothing he does is good enough, then you want to start encouraging him. Give him lots of praise; make sure you don't put yourself or others down in front of him. Don't set your standards so high that he feels discouraged. Get him involved in outside activities that he enjoys: sports, art, music, and so on.

Q. My ten-year-old gets into fights with my five-year-old. How should I handle the discipline? Do I give time-outs to both kids?

A. Yes. Give a time-out of ten minutes to the older child and five minutes to the younger child. Make sure that the children are in separate areas—not facing each other.

Q. What do I say when my friend gives her six-year-old boy a spanking? I put my son on time-out.

A. Tell your son that every family disciplines differently. Do not tell him that what his friend's mother does is "bad." You might want to discuss time-out with this boy's mother, but be respectful of other parents' philosophies.

Q. My husband feels time-out should be used only in the house. He is not comfortable using it in public places. I disagree. What do you say?

A. In order for time-out to be effective, it must be used consistently. If your child knows that you won't use time-out in public places, he may misbehave knowing that there will be no consequences. Discipline is not an "in-house" tool. Use it everywhere.

Q. My seven-year-old son will *not* stop biting other children. I have tried using time-out, but nothing works. What do you suggest I do?

A. Your son may have a problem that cannot be altered behaviorally by time-out. You may need to seek professional help if the biting continues. The biting may be a manifestation of a more serious problem.

Q. My kids are *always* fighting over toys and TV programs. I'm tired of being a referee. What should I do?

A. Here is a good opportunity to use the timer. Set it for an appropriate amount of time, and let each child take turns. When the timer "dings," it is time to change toys or TV stations. Most children are very responsive to a timer.

Q. My four-year-old son is very hyperactive. He has a tough time sitting and playing for any length of time. Do you think something is wrong, or is this age-appropriate?

A. Many four-year-old boys are extremely active but not necessarily hyperactive. There is a fine line, and you need to distinguish between the two. I suggest observing your son's behavior over a period of time. Can he sit and watch a video or TV program? Can he sit at dinner or play with a toy for at least fifteen minutes? Is he easily distracted? Can he follow directions? When your child is with others his age, does he seem to be more active? If after close observation and assessment you still feel that your child appears hyperactive and unfocused, take him to your pediatrician or a child psychologist for a professional evaluation.

Q. My child has been diagnosed with Attention Deficit Disorder (ADD). Does that mean I can still use time-out?

A. Absolutely. Usually children with ADD thrive on structure and limits. A consistent use of time-out will help provide just that. I emphasize the word *consistent* because an ADD child will push past his boundaries unless he knows that he will be disciplined.

Q. When I reprimand my six-year-old daughter, she gets angry and says, "I hate you." I am extremely upset by this. What should I do?

A. It is OK for your daughter to be angry and express her feelings, but it is *not* OK for her to say she "hates you." Teach her more appropriate words for her feelings; for example, she can say, "I am angry," "I don't like you right now," or "You upset me."

You are the key player in your child's discipline. Sharing other parents' questions and concerns about parenting can help you to better understand some of the problems you may face in raising your child.

Epilogue

Observations and Personal Experiences

Every time I write a parenting book, I look at the struggles and triumphs in raising my own child. I try to learn from each new parenting experience. I have made many mistakes, and I have had to start over, wondering "What am I doing wrong?" In my books I try to share with other parents all of the best of what I have learned, because I believe we are all in this parenting process together.

I applaud and encourage all parents. You are doing the most exciting and challenging work of your life—raising a child. I applaud your caring, your efforts, your struggles, and your willingness to learn, to teach, to inform, to make mistakes so you can find your way and try again. Your efforts will inevitably help your child become a magnificent adult.

When you realize some of your discipline techniques aren't working right and you look for alternative ways to parent, you are sending a positive message to your child. You are saying "I want to help you. I want to be a more effective parent so that you can be a happier, more well-behaved child."

I asked my own ten-year-old recently how she would discipline her child when she grows up. She said, "Mom, I would use time-out because it isn't mean and doesn't hurt. I'd love my children, and I don't want to hurt them. But if my kids still didn't listen, I would take away going to McDonald's for a month and not let them watch TV." I felt satisfied that my discipline methods had sunk in. She actually realized the benefits and applied them to herself.

You may not always be 100 percent effective, and some of the methods in my book might work better with one child's temperament than with another's. But time-out has proven to be a saner, safer, more loving way to discipline a child than other techniques have. It serves a two-fold purpose: time-out helps both the child and the parent. It diffuses anger and conflict. It helps you and your child find a way to stop, *think*, and communicate. Open communication is the key to a good parent-child bond.

If parents hit their children, they not only are hurting the little ones physically but also hurting them mentally. They are sending out a message about violence. Eventually, if a parent continues to hit a child, he will think it is OK to hit back, that violence is acceptable. Certainly we live in a world that promotes violence all too often, so any technique that veers away from violence is better.

Time-out also promotes good communication. Instead of reacting to your child, you are placing the responsibility for his behavior with him.

For a healthy, happy child, I prescribe using time-out and the discipline techniques that accompany it.

Index

About the Author

Donna G. Corwin is the author of several parenting psychology books, including the best-selling *Time-Out for Toddlers* (now in its tenth printing), *Growing Up Great,* and *The Challenging Child*—all published by Berkley Books. She has written hundreds of articles for major magazines on parenting issues, health, travel, and lifestyles.

She lives in Beverly Hills, California, with her husband, Stan, and their daughter, Alexandra.